THE VIRGINIA WAY

THE VIRGINIA WAY

Photographs by Wolfgang Roth
Text by Guy Friddell
Published by Burda GmbH

To Jefferson's Virginians

"I have been planning what
I would shew you:
a flower here, a tree there;
yonder a grove, near
it a fountain; on this side a
hill, on that a river.
Indeed, madam, I know
nothing so charming as our
own country."

*Thomas Jefferson, to Mrs. Angelica
Church, in London, Feb. 17, 1788.*

Publisher:
DR. FRANZ BURDA

Layout:
Heinz Roßkopf

Production:
Heinz Morstadt
Werner Wieber
Heinz Vetter

Imprimatur:
Kurt Kläger

Layout-Assistence:
Kurt Lehr
Jan Bernd Nienborg
Karl-Heinz Steuer

Pictures on page 140/141, 166/167,
187: Virginia State Travel Service;
170/171: Thomas A. Defoe;
210/211: William Abourjile

© 1973 by BURDA GmbH,
Offenburg
Printed in West Germany

Contents

A state of bliss

You have heard, if you have been in the Commonwealth as much as a day, persons say, with a smile, a sigh, or a glint of pride in the eye, "Well, that is the Virginia way of doing things!"

Is there truly a Virginia way?

Numerous observers testify to it, including so perceptive a one as T. S. Eliot.

To cross to Virginia, the poet said, was "almost as definite as to cross the English Channel."

Of course, the Virginia way varies from generation to generation, even hour to hour; but certain constants persist, though at times one tradition may contest and supersede another.

To begin, then, consider a story told around the Capitol about Governor Fitzhugh Lee, Robert E. Lee's nephew, who won the Governorship in 1885.

The first elevator, pulled by ropes, was installed in the State House during Governor Lee's administration. When the contraption was reported ready for use, the Governor, a man of great girth and good humor, sent word to the local Commonwealth's Attorney to hurry over, he had a question on a weighty matter.

The Commonwealth's Attorney, who weighed 350 pounds, came panting into the Chief Executive's office and asked what was the question.

"Did you have any trouble on that elevator?" inquired the Governor.

Virginians, then, ordinarily are not averse to someone else trying a thing first.

But on occasions, and great ones, they have so acted that the Nation relied on them.

In 1776 when the struggle for independence was beginning, John Adams wrote Patrick Henry: "We all look up to Virginia for examples."

And at times, of course, even when many Virginians are inclined to do nothing about a matter, a few restless souls among them are harassing the lethargic majority.

Such an agitator was Captain John Smith trying to keep the Virginia experiment going.

Writing to England for reenforcements, Captain Smith begged: "When you send againe I entreat you rather send but thirty carpenters, husbandmen, Gardiners, fishermen, blacksmiths . . . than a thousand such as we have."

Evidence of Virginians' progressive instinct has surfaced in times more recent than the Revolution. In 1970 they approved a thoroughly revised State Constitution when voters elsewhere in the Nation were rejecting reforms. The new charter provided, among other advances, a mandate for schooling of high quality for every Virginia child.

Among those engaging in the autumn campaign for the revisions was Lieutenant Governor J. Sargeant Reynolds, who had been stricken in August with a brain tumor. During the few months remaining in his life he compiled a legacy of courage. In his initial statement from the hospital, he expressed more concern for Virginia's fate than his own: "May we settle our petty differences of color and background and go on with the challenge of achieving the highest form of human dignity for people everywhere."

Appearing at a noon-time rally in Capitol Square on October 22, seven weeks after his first hospital stay, Reynolds reminded the throng around the Bell Tower that "in the past the people of Virginia have acted boldly when the time has come to act boldly."

The young Lieutenant Governor was correct. But Virginians are adept as well at doing a thing so that the effect will not be appreciably greater than had they done nothing at all.

Consider how deftly the General Assembly handled the controversial issue of the sale of liquor.

When prohibition was repealed across the Nation in 1933, Virginians, wary of possibilities of corruption, approved the sale of liquor by the

Virginia's Capitol, designed by Thomas Jefferson, crowns a shady square in Richmond. Behind it are gray former City

10

Library with pyramidal roof, cross-shaped Medical College of Virginia Hospital and blue-paneled MCV teaching unit.

11

A state of bliss

bottle through stringently regulated State stores. In 1962 advocates arose for liquor-by-the-drink, promising an influx of tourists to bolster the economy. Drys, resisting fiercely, predicted an era of public drunkenness unparalleled in Virginia history, with a saloon on every corner.

After nearly a decade of public hearings, the General Assembly in 1968 gave the localities the option of deciding the question. But during the years that the bill had been bottled in committee, the legislators had devised an array of safeguards – a restaurant serving drinks had to have 50 seats, had to offer full meals, had to be lighted to a certain degree – so that the bill's passage produced neither the fabulously cosmopolitan atmosphere envisioned by the wets nor the skid prophesied by the drys. Things went along pretty much as before.

Virginia had found a way to take its drink, and not have it, too.

The bill's sponsor, Norfolk Delegate Bernard Levin, said that five years after its adoption people were coming up to him and asking if he thought Virginia would ever have liquor by the drink.

There are Virginia ways of saying things.

In fact, distinctions in pronunciations are so sharp from region to region that a person blindfolded could guess his whereabouts.

There is the brisk, yet casual fashion with which residents of the Star City refer fondly to "Ro-noke". With rugged individualists, it even becomes "Ru-noke".

Despite television's leveling impact on many differences in American life, it scarcely will iron out the wrinkles in Virginians' speech.

For a while a new resident persists in articulating Rowa-noke but, given time, he succumbs to the easy shorthand and suddenly concedes that he, too, is in Ro-noke.

Across the State in Portsmouth a newcomer is struck by the residents' habit of inserting the letter "h" in their city's name to make it Porchmouth.

When the newcomer taxes them about what seems an affectation, they look bewildered.

"Can't you say Ports-mouth?" asks the newcomer.

"That's what I said – Porchmouth," says the native.

Even more annoying to the newcomer, the day comes when, as he converses with friends from another region, they suddenly say, "Hey, what's that funny way you're pronouncing Portsmouth?"

Similarly, Isle of Wight citizens slip in an "h" to turn their county to Isle of White.

In Southwest Virginia, visitors are captivated by the treatment the residents give the letter "i", beginning as if they are going to change the "i" to "ah", but just before the vowel deepens to a broad "a", gliding with the "i" to a landing on the word's final consonant. When they say good naahiit in Big Stone Gap, night falls ever so slowly.

There is no way to convey the long-drawn "i" on paper, but the speech out there is a soft, soothing chant, worth going to hear.

On tiny Tangier Island, the inhabitants are adept at the tripthong. An ordinary, everyday hat becomes a beguiling higher-yet.

Through middle Virginia the ow-oo-ut flourishes, not so much a drawl as a quick dip, a curtsey; plain "about" becomes a-be-oot.

A Virginia girl playing Lady Macbeth – Ow-oo-ut! Ow-oo-ut! day-um-m-m spaw-woot! – would never get out the line, much less the spot.

Virginians' conservatism is rooted in the land.

No other state has a more varied face.

The Old Dominion, a triangle, is divided into three roughly equal parts of tidewater, piedmont, and mountains, laced by creeks and rivers.

Catch the diversity of Virginia's environment by glancing first at the triangle's corners.

At the apex around Washington, D.C. are teeming, towering "new towns" that sprang into existence in mid-twentieth century.

In the Southwest is the broad, ruffed-up carpet of ageless mountains that out-time time. See the mountains in the dusk or under dark clouds, fold on fold filling the horizon, gradations of gray and black fading into mistiness. This was the way the pioneers saw them after a long day of pushing along the Wilderness Road, and at the sight of the ranges looming they felt exaltation at their immensity and dispair at ever conquering them.

Mountain dwellers are aware almost constantly of the weather, the changes in the time of day, and the seasons' altering touch on the countryside. In the city a person has no notice of approaching rain; he only knows it's there when it's falling straight out of the sky onto his head. In the mountains the elements move on a broad canvas for all to see, and during a thunderstorm when shafts of sunlight stab through the clouds and strike the earth, the viewer feels he is seeing things at the start with the Lord separating light from darkness.

Across the base of the triangle to the east is the bustling Hampton Roads complex: Norfolk-Portsmouth, the Capital of the Navy, and Newport News, the Navy's builder. In the City of Chesapeake there is a good portion of the State's most celebrated swamp, Old Dismal; and at the foot of the Atlantic Ocean that brought us here is Virginia's sand pile, Virginia Beach.

A stir of excitement runs through Norfolk's waterside office buildings when a major ship enters or leaves the harbor.

To watch an aircraft carrier leave the Norfolk Naval Shipyard in Portsmouth where it has been undergoing repairs, and make its way slowly down the suddenly shrunken Southern Branch of the Elizabeth River, as if a chunk of land had broken off and is sliding away, is to see an unfolding scene too vast for the widest screen. The carrier, extending for blocks, crowds the Branch, and when it eases out into the Elizabeth River, the great ship seems to take Norfolk's skyline on its broad back, bearing a city out to sea while row on row of tiny pleasure boats in the Portsmouth marina marvel at its mighty passage, assisted by a tough little red tug.

At the fall line in the piedmont is the triangle's most distinguished structure, the State Capitol. Designed by Jefferson, the State House crowns 12 sloping, tree-clad acres in the heart of downtown Richmond.

Virginians feel at ease in Capitol Square's greenery, statuary, fountains, and winding walks. At noon secretaries from surrounding skyscrapers spread their lunches on the lawn under the Capitol's benign white brow. As they picnic they gaze upon a statue of Edgar Allan Poe, who wrote of a raven, sitting pensively amid pigeons.

In the block below the Capitol along Main Street is Richmond's financial district, a congeries of glossy, glassy structures sprouting thickset as seed warts, overtopping Capitol Square. From one pinnacle, Bull and Bear Club diners look down on the picnickers on the lawn and at Mr. Jefferson's enduring statement of good taste.

Ask a Virginian which region he prefers, and he is apt to reply, "I like it right here."

The loveliest in Virginia is where you are.

But there is more to the land than beauty.

In the beginning it meant independence.

Finding himself at odds with his neighbors, his employer, or himself, a man could move and start again. For a few pennies an acre he could buy a new life and shuck off his old self. Starting out in Southwest Virginia, Daniel Boone had a simple test: "I think it time to remove when I can no longer fall a tree for fuel so that its top will lie within a few yards of my cabin."

In Northern Neck you hear about John Ball, a cantankerous fellow who invariably fought on court day. One Saturday the Judge warned that the community could stand no more disruption, and he was putting him under a peace bond.

John stalked out under the court house portico, called the people around him, and announced that he was going to sell his farm next court day and move. They protested that he couldn't be serious, but he snapped he meant every word of it.

"Comes time a man can't fight in peace in this country I'm moving out!" he said.

Jefferson encouraged the notion that men were better for being closer to the land; "Those who labor in the earth are the chosen people of God, if ever He had a chosen people..."

(That statement came early in Jefferson's career. Later when he ran for President, he began to discover considerable merit in the residents of New England's mill towns.)

Somehow a man who wrested a living from the soil was reckoned more reliable than one who punched a clock. To the agrarian, a person who matches wits with nature and does the work himself is in closer touch with reality, nearer to the source, than another who shuffles papers at a desk or tightens bolts on an assembly line. After all, the land came first – and will again should we have to start over.

The Virginian cherishes even after he leaves the farm (often, more especially after he has left) country sights, sounds, and smells: katydids in the corn shocks, a creek brawling over rocks, the soft azure flare of a bluebird on a gray rail, the warm, heartening fragrance – it puts life into you, as if you are eating the very fields in which the grain grew – of corn bread baking on an iron skillet. Is there anything, come right down to it, much better than hot corn bread crumbled in cold milk?

Here, the Virginian thinks, standing with his feet on the ground, or in his imagination, is reality. A young woman, talking amid a tinkling cocktail party in Norfolk, confides that she will be revisiting mountainous Southwest Virginia soon. "I've got to go back," she says, "to find who I am."

All this found expression in an anguished bellow by State Senator Charles T. Moses of Appomattox, Buick dealer, and erstwhile farm lad. Feeling the country boys' power ebbing under court-ordered reapportionment in the 1962 General Assembly, Senator Moses bawled to his colleagues: "The reins of government should rest in the hands of those that turn the soil and slop the hogs!"

(He need not have fretted. On issues posing conflicts between cities and counties, such as merger and annexation, the suburban legislators were disposed to side with the rural boys – the hand that steered the power mower joining the hand that drove the tractor in circumventing the cities, even as rural poor were migrating to urban slums. But, generally, the reapportionment that gave more representation to the cities helped stimulate more progressive and responsive sessions of the General Assembly.)

Moses and Jefferson would be dismayed at statistics compiled by Edwin E. Holm, research director for State Industrial Development.

Dr. Holm found three long-term trends shaping Virginia's economy: decline of those employed in agriculture, the rise of factory workers, and spectacular growth in Federal military and civilian jobs. Of the three, the most persistent trend has been the dwindling number of farm workers.

At the century's turn, roughly one-half of all Virginians were engaged in agriculture. By 1970 only 3 per cent were so engaged. From a peak of 300,000 in 1920, employment in agriculture declined to 53,000 in 1970.

Virginia's rapid growth has been a phenomenon of recent decades, Dr. Holm found. Of the 18 states in the Union at the time of the first Census of 1790, Virginia was far and away the largest in

Shafts of sunlight pierce low-hanging clouds over mountain ridges in Southwest Virginia. Between the Blue Ridge an

gheny Mountains lies Virginia's Great Valley through which the pioneers traveled to North Carolina and Kentucky.

A state of bliss

population. But then for a century and a half it was one of the slowest growing states as Virginians left for better jobs elsewhere.

"The depression decade of the thirties was pivotal as Virginia grew at a rate substantially above the National growth rate. During the past three decades – the forties, the fifties, and sixties – Virginia has continued to grow in population at rates above the National average. For the decade of the sixties, Virginia's 17.2 per cent rate of growth was 30 per cent above the rate for the Nation."

During the 1970s the State's total population will increase by at least 800,000. Looking ahead to the year 2000, Professor H. Grant Goodell, environmental scientist at the University of Virginia, figured that Virginia, if it merely keeps pace with the national growth, will add a population equivalent to nine cities the size of Richmond.

Prospect of a population in excess of 7 million Virginians in less than 30 years requires vision and planning worthy of a Jefferson if any of Virginia's free and easy style of living is to be saved.

The solution calls for a delicate balancing of interests. For instance, a legislative committee planning to decentralize units of the outmoded State Penitentiary in Richmond was admonished by environmentalists not to establish a prison facility anywhere within four miles of an historic shrine.

But that policy, the legislators protested, would put the entire State of Virginia out of bounds. And anyway the Penitentiary itself was in a fair way to becoming an antique. Portions of it were standing when Lafayette revisited Virginia on his Farewell Tour in 1824.

In an interesting turnabout, some conservatives and liberals have swapped sides on the issues of population growth and industrial development.

In the early 1950s liberal leaders accused the Byrd Organization of discouraging industry, so as to keep wages low and organized labor weak. About the time the Harrison Administration started a drive in 1958 for new plants, ecologists began alerting the public to the dangers of industrial development. By the mid-1960s some liberals were becoming as dubious about growth as they had charged the conservatives with being earlier.

What's so often confounding for either side in public life is that the other, in retrospect, is proved right – if for the wrong reasons.

History is humbling, or ought to be.

Whatever the reasons, Virginia is in a more advantageous position than any other state on the East Coast to rescue its shore line from the bulldozer and keep its streams clean.

Our inertia has saved us.

But only for a spell.

The chance to leave to the next generation the environment Virginians love is fading.

For Virginians to keep the best of their heritage intact demands a healthy expenditure of energy.

But investments in providing parks and preserving wilderness and planning habitable cities will multiply in cash value as well as in the larger, intangible benefits to the people.

To stay the same, old Virginia must change.

In Virginia the land has produced, among other crops, a bounty of conversation. Life on the farms was attuned to the seasons' slow wheeling. Virginia hospitality traces to the time when each plantation, an isolated world, was famished for company. Some planters even waylaid strangers on the road and brought them home for conversation. Food was plentiful, talk rare, and the hosts clung to their callers. Scheherazade never would have finished spinning yarns in Colonial Virginia. At best she simply would have been passed from one great house to another. Odysseus, detained in Fluvanna, never would have regained Ithaca.

Time moved as slowly through the seasons as a great mill grinding the grain of conversation, sifting it fine, polishing it and the stories. It still does in many places in Virginia. A hearer who has heard a tale before, listens closely nevertheless, beginning to chuckle at the start, even moving his lips slightly as he stays in step with the narration, savoring nuances, exploding in mirth at the finish. It is a shared experience from first to last syllable. After all, if a person can derive pleasure from seeing a well-produced play or movie several times, why not hear a story repeatedly?

Life, to the Virginian, is a stage on which he is both actor and spectator. The stories are not so much jokes as they are commentaries on the show, especially the ruefulness of it. When a Virginian says, "Stop me if you've heard this!" it is an invitation to open, not close, communication.

Humor helped sustain them through the Civil War. In the Valley of Virginia, still making the rounds, is the account of a mother whose two sons, John and Jim, were in the Battle of Seven Pines. When word of fighting near Richmond reached her ears, she prayed for John night and day until finally her husband reminded her, "Jim's down there, too."

"Yes," she said, "but I know if there are seven pines, Jim is behind one of them!"

In early May watch Virginians at the annual shadplanking in the woods near Wakefield. While the shad, split open and nailed to a plank, is baking to a golden turn over beds of coal, some 3,000 men are sipping bourbon, listening to the political speeches (heard, really, by only the 50 nearest the platform), and, most of all, telling stories. It sounds as if a flock of starlings has lit in the grove.

See three or four men talking together, drifting about as if treading water as they talk, touching elbows, then straying six feet away, coming back close, bending their heads to catch the punch line of the story, then exploding apart again, guffawing, slapping their knees, grabbing at their stomachs in a paroxyism of mirth, bounding back this time at such great distances, that one or another is caught on the rebound in another floating circle and falls to repeating the story. In that way it wriggles through the woods at Wakefield and from there throughout Virginia, a live thing.

On such boisterous occasions old Senator Harry F. Byrd relished hearing how his assistant, M. B. "Peachey" Menefee, had fared in his political career years before he came to work for Byrd.

For three terms young Menefee was Commissioner of Revenue for Page County in the Shenandoah Valley, and one year, running for re-election, he went into an auto repair shop at a crossroads and approached the owner, who was working on his back under a flivver, only his feet extending into view. Bending slightly, incumbent Menefee called, "I wonder if you'd support me for Commissioner of Revenue?"

"Hell, yes," came back the voice from under the car. "I'd vote for anybody before I'd vote for that damn fool!"

Much of Virginians' celebrated absorption with the past simply is an interest in life as a vast continuing sequel with a cast of characters running into thousands and a plot full of more ramifications and improbable coincidence then even Charles Dickens could imagine.

Sprawl on the sand in the sun at Virginia Beach and listen to two women conversing nearby, the murmur of their voices, not gossiping, really, but catching up – which generally means going back, establishing connections, discussing family and friends, who married whom, where they live, the names and natures of their children, where they go to school, who they go with. If the two happen to be strangers, then the exploratory ritual is a way of getting acquainted. Exclamations of delight when they discover they have a mutual friend is almost as animated as if the third party suddenly had been conjured before them in the flesh.

Their talk is like a game of double solitaire, a placing of names in order, putting aside for a moment one that doesn't fit, falling to discussing now the two leading families with Virginia-born Bishops in the Episcopal Church, concluding after long enumeration and cross references that the Kinsolvings have the lead by one Bishop, but there are more Tuckers coming on – and, oh! – there's the name they couldn't recollect, and, placing it on the proper pile, they have opened up a whole new run of cards to distribute. They go on murmuring happily, laughing a little for some exploit, indulging in a soothing chant, so that with the susurrus of the sea in the background, the glare of the sun on one's eyelids, and the warmth of the sand on the back, listening to the pleasant chatter of women playing social solitaire, one sleeps.

In pursuit of the past, Virginians have marked their land until it bristles with signs and plaques.

They mark birthplaces, death beds, offices, homes, churches, creeks, courthouses, battlefields, rivers, hills, valleys, and a sycamore tree in which a pioneer father and his two sons spent the night.

Virginians, if they could, would mark the air.

Master marker of them all was William E. Carson, first Chairman of the Virginia Conservation and Development Department under Governor Harry Byrd. He devised a system of historic roadside markers – yard-square metal tablets, with black block lettering embossed on a silver background – mounted on poles. To the traveler the Commonwealth seems to be a giant history book, page after page unfolding with the turning road.

In Henrico Country are 32 markers charting the course of the Seven Days' Battle during which Lee's Army of Northern Virginia drove back McClellan's forces from Richmond.

In Fairfax and Prince William Counties the motorist has to stay abreast of both the First and Second Battles of Manassas swirling around him silently over the same terrain, one occurring at the beginning, the other midway through the Civil War. Not even Robert E. Lee had to keep track of two battles simultaneously.

In 1927 when Chairman Carson turned loose his crew to begin marking the Commonwealth, automobiles traveled at 25 to 30 miles an hour or, through mud and ruts a good deal less, so that a motorist had time to contemplate signs of the past; but now, whipping by at 60, the viewer has only a fleeting impression that NEAR HERE, ON MATRIMONY CREEK... or FROM THIS VICINITY WENT FORTH... or ON THIS ROAD LAFAYETTE... or IN THE GROVE TO THE NORTHWEST ... something happened.

Or his eye may catch a tantalizing title: THE MUD MARCH ... A GREAT PREACHER ... THE SERVANT'S PLOT ... THE LAST FIGHT ... BROTHER AGAINST BROTHER ... WRECK OF THE OLD 97 ... LEE'S LAST CAMP.

They blip by, and if the motorist does not pause to read and ruminate, he will one day. Meanwhile he is aware he is in a thicket of history.

Among the markers thronging Virginia is one at Front Royal honoring William E. Carson for establishing, among other things, the markers.

Along with the talking the land allowed time for reading, writing, and speculating on grand topics, with impressive results in some of the Revolutionary War leaders.

And that creative era, trumped by a haunting lost cause, accounts in part for Virginians' interest in the past. In the space of a few square miles – Jamestown–Williamsburg–Yorktown – were major acts in the Nation's building and maturing. Then, having been so much a part of the founding, Virginia became the main scene in the attempted undoing, from First Manassas to the collapse at

The supercarrier Forrestal, the first of its class, moves after repairs at the Naval Shipyard in Portsmouth down the Eliza

r on its way to the Norfolk Naval Station. In the foreground is a marina in Portsmouth. Norfolk's skyline rises in the rear.

Appomattox. Now, at the prompting of the Federal Courts, the Commonwealth again is out front, desegregating public schools, and, thanks to the Virginia people's good sense, setting in the main a constructive example for other states.

Meanwhile, the visitor to Virginia may be bemused by the jostling of past and present. No sooner does he leave Byrd International Airport in Richmond than he spies meandering mounds, as if some giant mole has passed by, and a sign: DON'T WALK ON THE TRENCHES.

That essentially was what Confederates were telling Yankees for four years. In Virginia they fought more than 1,000 battles, engagements, and skirmishes, accounting for 60 percent of the Civil War. One does not lightly lay aside such burdens.

Old soldiers as they sat under tall oaks amid silent cannon remembered famished Confederates charging through an orchard into Federal guns at Sharpsburg and grabbing apples and devouring them as they ran at the Yanks . . . two Confederate divisions holding a snowball battle on the heights over Fredericksburg while they waited for the Federals to attack, and, when General Burnside threw his Union troops at the heights, slaughtering Yankees until the plain below was draped in blue cloth . . . soldiers amid point-blank firing at the Bloody Angle placing the hand of a corpse so that, when it stiffened, it would hold their cartridges.

In courthouse squares and graveyards, Virginians raised more than 1,000 monuments to the Confederate dead, and, so doing, sought to ease their anguish at remembering. To begin to forget, to fold away the past, they first had to pay it tribute and remember.

In the White House of the Confederacy is a recollection by Jennie D. Harrold. She recalled going as a child with a young woman who was taking a basket "of good Hanover provisions" to a sick soldier friend in a camp hospital. But when they arrived they found he had died that morning and been buried in Hollywood Cemetery. At Hollywood they followed directions of those in charge and found on a little wooden headboard over a fresh grave an inscription:

"I leave my boy at 5. A.M. for my North Carolina home. His father."

At the unveiling of Lee's recumbent statue at Washington and Lee University, John Daniel. Lame Lion of Lynchburg, spoke three hours.

After the Lion finished, even the most inveterate ex-Confederate must have felt he had done his duty, that day, anyway.

Even now Virginia's leaders are wont to call shades of great Virginians. Indeed, addressing an audience at Woodrow Wilson's birthplace in Staunton, Governor Mills Godwin Jr. began by observing gravely, "I know of nothing Virginians do in which they excel any more than in paying tribute to their own."

A ripple of laughter spread through the audience at the Governor's unexpected bull's-eye at Virginians' readiness to praise one another.

Nobody ever outdid John Jasper, a Negro evangelist, in extoling Virginians.

"There are four races of men," he said, "Huguenots, Abyssins, Hottentots, and Virginians."

"And Virginians," he added, "are the only race that doesn't have to be born again!"

In a famous sermon — he preached it 241 times — the former slave also asserted that "the sun do move."

Virginians, ever eclectic, do not find it difficult to admire the first proposition while reserving some doubt on the second.

(Jasper argued from the Bible that if the sun stopped at the command of Joshua during the battle of Jericho, then it must have been moving, for "nothin' kin stop untel it has fust startid . . . It stopt fur bizniz, an' went on when it got through . . .")

If one trait characterizes John Jasper's Virginians, it is a sense of decency, which has enabled them to come through troubled times in fair calm with some grace.

They expect two qualities in their leaders and government: courtesy and honesty. The first is akin to the good humor that Thomas Jefferson urged on his 15-year-old grandson as the best "preservative of peace and tranquillity." The second is basic to any government's fair dealing with the people.

As for John Jasper, he learned to read from an old slave, became converted while stemming tobacco in a Richmond factory, and after the Civil War started a church in a shanty on an island in the James River. He and his followers built the Sixth Mount Zion Baptist Church, a red brick structure on the northeast corner of Duval and St. John's Streets. Jasper preached the church out of debt with his famous sermon, which he delivered for the first time on March 28, 1879. Once offered a hefty sum to go to London, the tall, commanding shepherd declined to forsake his flock.

During Jasper's 36 years as pastor, both races flocked to hear him, including so many Richmond College ministerial students that they became known as "Jaspers".

Mount Zion now butts on the heavily traveled Richmond-Petersburg Turnpike. Twentieth century members, steadfast as their founder, refused to sell the church to make way for the toll road. It, like the sun, had to move.

Jasper's celebrated sermon defended the Bible against doubts arising in the scientific age. Whether the sun moves or not made no difference to him, he said, so long as the Bible prevails as "a guide that will tell us what we got to do, conduct us through this life, and lead us into heaven."

And, after all, is it so extravagant to assert that the sun do move in a State where, now and then, the blessed inhabitants behave as if time stood still?

Where it all began

A visitor going below decks on the three tiny ships moored at Jamestown's shore has the sensation of entering a child's cozy room ingeniously fitted like a ship's hold.

Did some 105 settlers, plus crews, actually buck the ocean in toys such as these replicas?

The first wonder is that they made it at all to Jamestown in 1607.

Astronauts, by contrast, travel in luxury, tethered to computers in the space control center.

The flagship, the Susan Constant, weighed only 100 tons; the Godspeed, 40 tons, and the Discovery, 20 tons. But they stayed afloat and managed, mysteriously moreover, to stay together on the four-month voyage.

On April 26, 1607, after a violent storm, the travelers sighted land and a party of 20 went ashore to explore and had their first brush with Indians. That night aboard ship Captain Christopher Newport opened a sealed chest which contained the Virginia Company's orders naming a governing council of nine. On April 29 they planted a large wooden cross on a cape they named for Prince Henry.

After beating about for two weeks, they hit upon a marshy island in the James River, as they named it. The little island could easily be defended, they reasoned. On May 14, with their "shippes ... moored to the Trees in six fathom water," they went ashore to found James Towne. They built a log palisade, 420 feet long on the river side and 300 feet on the other two sides, and started gardens.

They scarcely could have picked a worse spot in which to begin the experiment.

In the first place they had intruded on a powerful community of Indians.

If a settler came through what they called, grimly, a "seasoning" of diseases including malaria, scurvey, typhoid fever, dysentery, and pneumonia . . .

And if after the rain rotted the stores and the rats got in the grain, the settler still scraped together a fistful of food . . .

And if he escaped fires that burned the town . . .

He might live just long enough to be picked off by one of Powhatan's redmen lurking in the reeds.

Half the company were gentlemen and gallants – "roarers and loiterers" for the most part, John Smith said.

"The Starving Time," the terrible winter of 1609–10 after Captain Smith had returned to England, trimmed the population from 600 to 50.

(How they managed to starve amid so much plenty lying about – oysters, clams, crabs, nuts, berries, and what not – is another mystery. Maybe they just lacked Smith to point them out.)

In May, 1610, the Colony's lieutenant governor, Sir Thomas Gates, long delayed after his ship was wrecked in Bermuda, reached Jamestown. He agreed to carry the wasted survivors back to England, they abandoned Jamestown, and were sailing down the river when they received word that Lord de la Ware, the Company-appointed Governor, was coming with supplies. They turned back.

Had they fled Jamestown, the land would not long have remained unsettled. But failure at Jamestown would have meant an altogether different America, with no Washington to command a fight for independence, no Henry to fire men's emotions, no Jefferson to define their rights, and no Madison to fix them in a Constitution.

And the Colony would have died had it not been for a hardy few, especially the intrepid Smith and one other, an Indian child.

At 27 Smith already was a veteran of wars in the Netherlands and Eastern Europe. He arrived in the New World under arrest for some shipboard dispute. He never was one to suffer fools gladly, and an abundance of them was on the manifest. But the Virginia Company's instructions, opened

Three tiny sailing ships lie at anker off the James River's north shore in the beautiful Jamestown Festival Park. The

...as of the Susan Constant, the Godspeed, and the Discovery that brought the 105 colonists from England in 1607.

at Cape Henry, named him to the Council, and the settlers elected him president.

To survive, of course, was the first objective, but as he went about the business of saving the Colony his purpose went beyond mere survival in his will to live intensely, all senses alert, in the raw and wonderful land.

Trading with Indians, punishing them when need be, putting the gentlemen to work ("He that will not worke shall not eate"), pouring a dipper of cold water down their sleeves when they shirked, exploring one after another the rivers that led so enticingly into the interior, mapping it all, he was carrying out the Virginia Company's orders, but really he was doing it for a John Smith eager to see what marvel the next bend of the river or top of the hill would disclose. The furiously energetic little Captain scorned those who hung whining around Jamestown and "never adventured to know anything."

On an expedition, spearing fish with his sword near the mouth of the Rappahannock River, he speared a stingray. It struck its poisoned barb nearly an inch and a half in Smith's wrist, and the Captain's hand, arm, and shoulders swelled so alarmingly that his companions gave him up for dead; but after four hours he recovered and triumphantly "ate of the fish for his supper."

After two years an accidental gunpowder explosion injured his leg and forced his return to England. Then he relived every adventure, even as he had devoured the stingray, by writing about it, offering maps and advice to those who settled New England. His accounts show him to be one of the first to love America for what she was, not for the gold he called fool's glitter, but for herself in all her incredible adversity.

An Elizabethan adept with pen and sword, he also was the first American, prophesying a new society, which, with abundant resources, could give each individual a chance to be his or her best self.

The reader today still catches the freshness of Smith's observations in the strange Aroughcun, much like a badger but living in trees; the Assapanick, a squirrel that flew; an Opassam that "hath an head like a Swine, and a taile like a Rat, and is of the bignes of a Cat" and under her belly "a bagge, wherein she lodgeth, carrieth, and suckleth her young. . . ."

Of all that John Smith beheld, nothing exceeded in wonder or matched in importance a girl of 11, Pocahontas.

She cartwheels on history's stage, frolicking about the stockade with the company's cabin boys. Powhatan's favorite daughter, impressionable, impetuous – her Indian name meant "wanton" or "playful" one – she was fascinated with the colonists and most especially the stocky little blue-eyed man who did not clap himself in the fort like a terrapin but roamed everywhere asking questions.

An expedition exploring the Chickahominy River brought John Smith to Pocahontas' arms. In December, 1607, he proceeded as far as he could in a barge, then pushed ahead in a canoe with two settlers and two redmen, and finally went on alone to hunt birds for food. He was captured by 200 Pamunkey Indians, who took him at his demand to their king, Opechancanough. The Captain gave the king an ivory pocket-compass, ex-

Tourists inspec[t] three ships at Festival Park

On May 14, 1607, after four months at sea on the Susan Constant, the Godspeed and Discove[ry] some 105 colonists landed on a mosquito-ridd[en] marshy island to found James Towne. They cut tre[es] built a three-sided fort on an acre of ground, started gardens, traded goods and blows with Chie[f] Powhatan's tribe, and barely survived the 'Starving Time.' The great experiment had begu[n]

24

Reconstructed palisade shows visitors how colonists lived

*Settlers mixed
mud and sticks to make
wattle-and-daub
shelters with timber frames
and thatched roofs.
Fort encloses 16 structures
in 'a faire row.'
Behind well, three soldiers
sit by guardhouse.
Children play with cannon
which settlers
used to repel Indians.
Others study stocks
in which men repented
for swearing
and for missing church.
In 1619, for six days,
22 burgesses gathered on
benches in church
and made laws in the first
English-speaking Assembly
in the New World.*

plained to the intrigued chief why he couldn't touch its face through the glass, pointed out the needle's pointing north, and then went into "a discourse of the roundness of the earth, the course of the sunne, moone, starres and plannets" – a true son of Elizabeth instructing a stone age ruler in the workings of the solar system.

After several weeks the Pamunkeys took Smith to Powhatan's seat at Werowocomoco on the York River in the present Gloucester County. From here the great chief reigned by force and guile over 30 tribes of 9,000 people in 161 arboreal villages.

Smith found Powhatan a forbidding figure, reclining on mats on a bedstead a foot high, women seated at his head and feet, chains of pearls about his neck, under "a great covering of Rahaughcums."

After a feast, Indians took hold of Smith, laid his head on two huge stones before the emperor, and were preparing to beat out his brains when Pocahontas rushed forward and "got his head in her armes, and laid her own upon his to save him from death."

Nor was that the first time she saved Smith and the Colony. She slipped through the wilderness to warn them of attacks by her father's braves and repeatedly brought food to the palisade. As long as she lived, the two races were at peace.

After the wound from the gunpowder explosion forced Smith's return to England, the colonists in 1613 kidnapped Pocahontas as a hostage. With her gift for making the best of any circumstance, she lived cheerfully among the English, took the name Rebecca after being baptized, and married John Rolfe. Rolfe's long and tedious letter asking Governor Thomas Dale's permission to marry Pocahontas says he would do it for the good of the plantation, the honor of England, the glory of God, his own salvation, and for the converting of an "unbeleivinge Creature, namely Pocahuntas," and at last gets to the heart of the matter by confessing that his "hart and best thoughtes are and have byn a longe tyme soe intangled & inthralled in soe intricate a Laborinth, that I was even awearied to unwynde my selfe thereout."

In 1616 the couple, their child Thomas, and a dozen Indians went with Governor Dale to England. Powhatan sent along his sage, Uttamatom, to discover whether John Smith's fabulous accounts of England were true, and, most of all, if John Smith was dead, as they had been told. (Uttamatom's plan was to take along a stick and make a notch for every Englishman he saw.)

John Smith came at last to see the Indian Princess who had saved his life nearly 10 years before. After a "modest salutation," he recorded, she turned away and hid her face. Smith and the others left her alone two or three hours. When the Captain returned, Pocahontas reminded him that he had promised Powhatan that "what was yours would

Statues honor man and maid who saved Jamestown

Captain John Smith enforced a simple command on lazy colonists: He that will not worke shall not eate. He explored and mapped rivers and met Pocahontas, who saved him from Powhatan, and saved the Colony from starving to death. She married John Rolfe, who planted tobacco and made the Colony prosper and grow. But Pocahontas loved Captain John Smith.

29

In mid-May a parade marks "Jamestown Day" where settlers founded colony

Every year at Jamestown on the second Sunday in the Governor, General Assembly, Association for Preservation of Virginia Antiquities, plus tourists, troop down an oyster-shell path to a wood cross. They watch a wreath placed on the communal grave of 75 who died during the Starving Time, 1609–10. Famine reduced the Colony from 500 souls to 60. The survivors boarded ship, and sailed for home, but heard help was coming, and turned back. All that is left standing at Jamestown. Is the brick church tower of 1639, a ruin open to the stars and to our questions.

be his, and he the like to you; you called him father, being in his land a stranger. And by the same reason, so must I do you."

The rush of words to bridge the years was as heart-felt and direct as had been the child's dash to shield the Captain from death. She brushed aside Smith's protest that she, a king's daughter, should not call him father.

Had he not, she asked, come into her father's country "and caused feare in him and all of his people and feare you here I should call you father? I tell you I will, and you shall call me child, and so I will be for ever and ever your Countrieman. They did tell me always you were dead, and I knew no other til I came to Plimouth; yet Powhatan did command Uttamatom to seeke you and know the trouth, because your Countrieman lie much."

In 1617 John Rolfe boarded ship with his family to return to Jamestown, but the vessel had not cleared the port of Gravesend before Pocahontas became fatally ill. Accepting death with the equanimity with which she had greeted all the other amazing turns in her short life, she told her husband: "All must die. It is enough the child liveth."

The child did, and through him, thousands.

The child that was the Colony also prospered, although in dealing with her people, it failed to follow her compassionate example.

Her trusting words — "for ever and ever your Countrieman" – come to us through the centuries, a reproach, a reminder, a summary of the way of a Virginian who tried to reconcile races and cultures.

No wonder poet Vachel Lindsay called her "the mother of us all."

John Rolfe, a kind of broker in history, made another major contribution by introducing a strain of mild tobacco that quickly proved to be the Colony's money crop.

John Smith, writing of the death of the 22-year-old Pocahontas, said, "Poor little maid. I sorrowed much for her thus early death, and even now cannot think of it without grief, for I felt toward her as if she were mine own daughter."

It never seems to have crossed his ordinarily perceptive mind that Pocahontas was in love with him.

The year 1619 was a turning point for the Colony. A new and progressive head of the Virginia Company of London, Sir Edwin Sandys, sent to Jamestown by Governor George Yeardley a proclamation calling for a general assembly that the people "might have a hand in governing themselves."

Sandys' Great Charter provided for the election of two burgesses from each of 11 "principal plantations" or settlements in the Colony now grown to 1,900 people. On July 30, 22 tobacco farmers met in Jamestown's wooden church for six days.

In 1624 the Virginia Company was dissolved. Virginia became England's first royal coloney, but the habit of self-government had taken hold of the planters. They continued meeting in the General Assembly. In 1639 Charles I instructed the Royal Governor to call "a General Assembly once a year" and thus sanctioned what Virginians were doing anyway.

Not long after the first Assembly adjourned, a ship controlled by the Earl of Warwick brought the first blacks, about 20 indentured servants, to Virginia. They earned their freedom; thousands who followed had no such chance.

That the blacks, torn from their country and separated from their families, survived at all was heroic. That they entered wholeheartedly in helping build the Nation in which they were so long denied full rights is self-sacrificial service unparalleled.

The third event that marked 1619 was the arrival of 90 "younge, handsome and honestly educated maydes," who would, the Virginia Company expected, exert a steadying influence.

The most explosive passage occurred in 1676 when a young planter, Nathaniel Bacon, led an insurrection against aged Governor William Berkeley. Their strife continues among historians trying to decide between the good guys and the bad guys. Berkeley and Bacon were forever swapping roles. Bacon, who began by asserting the colonists' right to defend themselves against Indian attacks, ended by launching unauthorized forays against friendly Indians and by burning Jamestown. Berkeley, closed by hanging two dozen rebels – and prompting King Charles II to observe: "The old fool has killed more people in that naked country than I have done for the murder of my father."

Bacon had his men pledge that they would follow him no matter what. He heartened them by crying: "Come on, my hearts of gold! He that dyes in the field lyes in the bedd of honour!"

(Bacon's Rebellion died with his death, probably of dysentery, in Gloucester. His grave is unknown, but a plaque in the Courthouse casts Bacon as "the Washington of his day," and Berkeley as a villain, whatever historians may say.)

A mile from the site of Jamestown is the Festival Park with replicas of the three ships, museums, and stockade. On a memorial is poet John Donne's assessment of the Colony: "You have made this Island, which is but the suburb of the Old World, a bridge and gallery of the New."

The relics at the original site are undisturbed. On the ground are the flat stone foundations of dwellings, as if traced by a child for a playhouse. Nearby is a cross marking a communal grave of 75 victims of "the Starving Time." Beyond are the ruins of the ivy-covered Old Tower, all that remains of the first brick church built in 1639.

The Tower's tall cavernous entrance looks like a keyhole to the past, which, if we could unlock, would disclose all the mysteries of our beginnings, where now there is but deep silence, patterned by shadows of green and gold leaves shifting in the sun.

"Go make tobacco"

When John Rolfe returned from England, his entrepreneurial eye must have glistened to see that the tobacco seed he had planted was flourishing. Indeed the Colonists were growing tobacco in Jamestown's streets. In a tawny leaf, they had found gold.

King James, for one, was displeased. He said so in language that anticipated the U.S. Surgeon General and indignant modern-day writers of letters to the editor. In a "Counterblaste to Tobacco" he criticized the Colonists for the "vile use" of that "precious stink . . ."

But too late. . . The weed had taken hold, and with it, the Colony. Just how tight a grip the plant had was evident in 1691 when the Virginia Assembly authorized Commissary James Blair to go to England and seek a charter for a proposed college. The King and Queen approved the grant, but Attorney General Edward Seymour, who had to draw the charter, balked.

But, argued Blair, the college would train ministers, and Virginians had souls that needed saving.

"Souls! Damn your Souls! Make Tobacco!" shouted Seymour.

Could King James have seen the consequences of Virginians' making tobacco along the creeks and rivers he would have been even more vehement in his attack. Along with all the vices he attributed to it, tobacco engendered in the Colonists a nasty addiction to independence which prompted them in time to break away from England's apron strings.

In a lively, scholarly work, *The Story of Tobacco in America,* Dr. Joseph C. Robert of the University of Richmond has termed the discovery that tobacco could be successfully grown and profitably sold "the most momentous single fact in the first century of settlement on the Chesapeake Bay."

The staple, writes Dr. Robert, "guaranteed the permanence of the Virginia settlement; created the pattern of the Southern plantation; encouraged the introduction of Negro slavery, then softened the institution; strained the bonds between mother country and Chesapeake colonies; burdened the diplomacy of the post-Revolutionary period; promoted the Louisiana Purchase; and after the Civil War, helped create the New South . . ."

Americans ordinarily think of their country's progress as leap-frogging from Jamestown to Williamsburg and the Revolution. But first the Colonists ventured up Virginia's creeks and rivers.

(In Virginia's Tidewater there is little difference between the two. Where Corotoman Creek joins the Rappahannock River, the site from which Robert "King" Carter directed 42 plantations and 300,000 acres, the creek is three miles wide. Other creeks in that vicinity are Hull Creek, half a mile wide, in Northumberland County, and Antipoison Creek and Dividing Creek in Lancaster County, also half a mile wide. Tidewater's creeks would make respectable rivers in Southwest Virginia.)

Up the creek or river a man cleared land on the bank and built a home that was his castle. The thought began taking root on these far shores that a man's castle was as good as a king's.

Instead of huddling like shopkeepers in a village, the planters spread apart. Each managed a little world of wharf, warehouses, store, shipyard, farm, and a dozen artisans. He was called upon to make incessant decisions. The habit of judgment he formed in running the plantation was put to work in directing the Colony through the church vestry, the court, and the elected House of Burgesses and the appointed King's Council. The planters built, along with their great houses, a gifted ruling class, and they cemented it with marriages. The families formed a close-knit kingdom along tidal rivers, the FFVs.

Their names flow through Colonial history – the Carters, Harrisons, Fitzhughs, Pages, Burwells, Ludwells, Nelsons, Beverleys, Masons, Carys, Wormeleys, Diggeses, Lees, Byrds – interlacing like the tributary creeks and rivers on which they lived.

Their saving grace was a sense of duty to public good. "It is not fine clothes nor a gay outsight," King Carter advised a grandson, "but learning and knowledge and virtue and wisdom that makes a man valuable." They exerted a massive, steady pressure against the King's Royal Governor; and they readied the stage for the appearance of the great libertarians in the 18th century's last quarter.

The greatest procession of plantations is along the James River, beginning with Carter's Grove, which Colonial Williamsburg is restoring under President Carlisle Humelsine as a working 18th century plantation. King Carter's grandson, Carter Burwell, began building the mansion in 1750. The paneled entrance hall frames a lordly carved stairway, up which, 'tis said, Colonel Banastre Tarleton, a British cavalryman, spurred his horse and, as he rode, hacked the railing with his sabre — an unmannerly exhibition, if true, and one not calculated to help the sabre. The notches are there yet.

Route 5 from Williamsburg to Richmond is known as Plantation Road. Its two winding lanes are wooded most of the way, stippled with brown trunks and black shadows, so that it could be a private drive for the signs that announce the great houses lying back in the woods: Berkeley, Shirley, Westover, President John Tyler's Sherwood Forest, Evelynton, Bel Air, and Bush Hill.

Shirley was built by Edward Hill III for his daughter Elizabeth, who in 1723 married John Carter, son of King Carter. Anne Hill Carter was born at Shirley and was married there to Light Horse Harry Lee. Among their children was Robert E. Lee, who, as a child, visited his mother's home.

Carter blood made Lee Lee, the Carter family likes to think. They probably are correct. There's evidence for that view in the sight of Lee's mother struggling to hold the family together while Light Horse Harry failed in nearly everything but leading cavalry.

If Robert E. Lee's love of soldering came from his father, his unbelievable coolness in battle probably stemmed from the Carters' vast equanimity.

The present Carters have a letter Lee wrote after the Civil War to his first cousin Hill Carter advising him: ". . . Work is what we all require, work by everybody, work especially by white hands" — Lee underlined *white*, thinking, as he wrote, of those who had relied so heavily on black hands — "We must spend less my dear cousin, Hill, than we formerly did. We must use that little sparingly and only purchase what is actually necessary. By this course the good old times of former days which you speak of will return again. We may not see them but our children will."

Catching sight of Shirley, a glowing rose structure with a double two-story porch and a forecourt of outbuildings, the visitor thinks of it first as a world to itself. On the river side, under a giant tree, is a massive rock, which seems in the shade to be a huge cushion. That the boulder was placed there in the

34

Off Route 5, the Plantation Road between Richmond and Williamsburg, rears rose-hued Shirley, shaded by trees above the lazy James River In its great hall hangs a portrait of "King" Carter in bright red coat.

His eldest son married Elizabeth Hill, who inherited Shirley. Their granddaughter was the mother of Robert E. Lee, who played as a child on the lawn of his mother's old plantation. In the house's rear are dependen- cies in a forecourt, so that, approaching, a visitor feels he is seeing a small world all to itself, which is what each Great Plantation was. Here the planter trained to manage a larger world, the Colony and a Nation.

Nine generations have lived in Shirley, durable as boulder on lawn

Great houses, tobacco-based, crown bluffs

In 1750 Carter Burwell, "King" Carter's grandson, began constructing Carter's Grove overlooking the James River (above). He took six years to finish the stately mansion. British cavalryman Banastre Tarleton is reputed to have hacked deep scars in balustrade (right) as he spurred up the stairs. Berkeley was the home of the Harrison family that produced two of the Nation's Presidents. Here the Yankees camped. General Butterfield composed "Taps" which floated over the river to the Confederates. Here also was Thanksgiving first held, 'tis said.

20th century might seem a reordering out of keeping with the house's past except that the owner, Hill Carter Jr., is a ninth generation member of the family, which makes any change a matter of continuity. Shirley's two-story uprightness, like a child's Christmas dollhouse, is appealing.

Nearby is Berkeley, the oldest three-story house in America. A Colonial leader, Benjamin Harrison, built it in 1726. His son, Colonel Benjamin Harrison, signed the Declaration of Independence, served in the Continental Congress, and was thrice Governor of Virginia.

Colonel Harrison's younger son, William Henry, was elected President of the United States and returned to Berkeley to write his inaugural address in the room in which he had been born. The Harrisons produced another President in Benjamin, grandson of William Henry.

During the Civil War General McClellan made Berkeley his headquarters. In 1862 General Butterfield composed taps there. Among the Union soldiers was drummer boy, John Jamieson, not then 14, who years later purchased the mansion with the idea of retiring there. His son, Malcolm, did a masterful job in restoring the old home and making the land productive.

It received, recently, a spate of public notice as the site of the first Thanksgiving two years before the Plymouth Rock festival. A Richmond lawyer, John J. Wicker Jr., doing research for a speech in 1958 in the Library of Congress, stumbled upon instructions ordering Colonists when they landed at Berkeley to set aside a day of Thanksgiving "which shall be observed every year perpetually." Wicker hurried with the information to Governor J. Lindsay Almond Jr.

"I noticed," Wicker said, "that as I told him the facts Lindsay was leaning forward across the desk, almost in my face. He said later he was trying to sniff my breath to see if I'd been drinking."

Wicker's early efforts at publicizing his cause were at half-time ceremonies at the Thanksgiving Day football game between the University of Richmond and the College of William and Mary. Accelerating, he put on a Colonial costume, knee breeches and all, and flew in 1961 to Massachusetts, where he presented bemused Governor John Volpe with a Virginia turkey. Then he wrung equal time in Thanksgiving Day proclamations from Presidents Kennedy and Johnson and a generous concession from historian Arthur B. Schlesinger Jr.

The Virginia Thanksgiving's most picturesque features have been Wicker's activities. Meanwhile, the Pilgrim fathers' progeny can, if they're a mind to, follow Virginians' custom and bill their Massachusetts feast as the oldest continuous Thanksgiving in the Western Hemisphere.

At stately Westover, a 24-room brick mansion crowning a bluff above the James, lived William Byrd II, who portrayed "His Great Self" and his time in secret diaries. Educated abroad, he returned to Virginia at the death of his father, a wealthy trader who left him 23,000 acres. He first married Lucy Parke, who inherited her father's celebrated temper. From Westover Byrd presided over a solar system of six plantations on the James and several other estates, totaling 177,000 acres.

Reading Byrd's diaries is like eating dried raisins off the stalk, dusty and pungent sweet, nourishing.

He arose at five nearly every morning and danced his dance, as he described his gymnastics, and then read a chapter of Hebrew and 200 lines of Greek. He was something of a food faddist – in addition to trying anything, he swore by certain dishes – he ate boiled milk for breakfast, and, as he walked about his domain, chewed frequently on the ginseng root, which, he wrote, "frisks the spirit beyond any other cordial."

He recorded his quarrels with the tempestuous Lucy – he objected to her plucking her eyebrows; she sulked at his talking at length in Latin to the parson – and the love-making that followed, once on the billiards table. (His second wife, whom Byrd married after Lucy died of smallpox during a visit to London, was Maria Taylor, of milder temperament. But even Maria became so excited over letters from England that she stayed awake all night, and so Byrd, when they arrived late in the day, found it necessary "to pocket them up until next morning."

He frequently invited the whole congregation to Sunday dinner and was hospitable to the Indians that appeared on Westover's broad lawns. He talked with Bearskin about his god, and he learned to swim Indian style, not striking out with both hands but alternating one hand after another "whereby they are able to swim both farther and faster than we do."

He went with naturalist Mark Catesby into the swamp to see a hummingbird's nest "with one young and an egg in it;" when it snowed, he ordered "drums of wheat to be thrown to the poor birds;" he dissected a muskrat, and he bombarded the Royal Society with his observations.

He led a party of 50 in surveying the boundary 241 miles between Virginia and North Carolina and wrote his spirited *The History of the Dividing Line* It contains his famous analysis of North Carolina as "Lubberland." He was equally satiric with Virginia. Of the Jamestown settlers, he wrote, "like true Englishmen, they built a church that cost no more than Fifty Pounds, and a Tavern that cost Five hundred."

For his day he was, biographers say, humane with his slaves, and felt that the British Parliament should consider ending "this unchristian traffic of making merchandise of our fellow creatures."

At one point in his diary, noting a muster of some county militia that he commanded, Byrd observed "Everybody respected me like a king."

He was a rare bird, Virginia's Black Swan.

Let's go to Williamsburg

In 1699 the legislators, who had been burned out of their fourth state house, gave up Jamestown at last as a bad site and moved the Capitol six miles inland to the Middle Plantation, which they renamed Williamsburg in honor of King William II.

Unlike miasmic Jamestown, Williamsburg is spread high and dry upon a ridge on a peninsula between two broad rivers. Spill a cup of water in the middle of the Duke of Gloucester Street, the costumed hostesses tell visitors, and half the contents would flow toward the James River and the other half to the York.

If the legislators found happiness in Williamsburg, then so do today's Virginians. Williamsburg is the salvation of Virginians when company comes from afar. What a relief to say, Oh, let's go to Williamsburg! — knowing that the guides, the movies, and the buildings themselves save a lot of explaining about the American Revolution and all that followed. Williamsburg offers instant, reconstituted history. At one spot on the Duke of Gloucester Street the visitor can, when trees are bare, see the Colonial town's five spires of power: the Wren Building of the College of William and Mary, the Governor's Palace, the Capitol, the Courthouse of 1770, and Bruton Parish Church.

The State Department also has caught the habit of letting Williamsburg do the entertaining. When dignitaries arrive from abroad, State whisks them by helicopter to the Colonial Capital for a day or two of restoration before entering twentieth century Washington. Virginia's Governor also relies on Colonial Williamsburg's expert staff to host such shows as the National Governors' Conference. The implication to the other states' governors is, oh, we live like this all the time, just plain old Virginia hospitality. Thus the town has resumed something of its role as the social, if not the political, capital of the Commonwealth.

Women especially bask in Williamsburg's well-ordered orbit. It's their idea of paradise. At no time in its past was the town at such a peak of perfection as it began to attain in 1926. In the old days the houses naturally reflected their owners' varying pocketbooks. So today's restorers let maintenance lag a little. Paint flakes on some buildings. A roof needs repairs. Grass grows long.

When the revival began, Restoration President Kenneth Chorley brought an old resident to vouch for a tavern's interior. The old-timer turned to where the bar should be — "There it is" — and then, looking around, he said, "Kenneth, it is much cleaner now."

Still, the Founding Fathers, always in pursuit of the ideal whether in little amenities or grand principles, would be pleased with the cared-for town.

Two men began the transformation. After a Phi Beta Kappa banquet at William and Mary, the Rev. W.A.R. Goodwin of Bruton Parish Church escorted John D. Rockefeller Jr. through the then dilapidated streets and suggested that the philanthropist resurrect an entire town. How that dignified pair must have enjoyed conspiring like boys on the project! Work began in 1926, and, half a century later, still goes on. The restoration's 50th birthday coincides with the Nation's 200th — cause, indeed, for the militia to fire a volley of joy.

No other place, no matter where, offers more to excite the mind than the 90 or so buildings clustered on 173 acres.

From Williamsburg George Washington set out to serve his apprenticeship in arms with the British in the French and Indian War. Of his baptism of fire, Washington wrote, "I heard the bullets whistle, and, believe me, there is something charming in the sound." (Reading the comment in a London magazine, King George II said, "He would not say so, if he had been used to hear many.")

In Williamsburg, a young lawyer defended a mulatto slave who was seeking his freedom. Under "the law of nature," the lawyer argued, "all men are born free, every one comes into the world with a right to his own person, which includes the liberty of moving and using it at his own will." The court dismissed the plea, but Thomas Jefferson never let go the proposition.

"The hand that writes this letter wrote the Constitution," James Madison late in his life advised a correspondent. Early, while Madison was a burgess in Williamsburg, the hand began learning legislative skills.

On May 29, 1765, wearing frontier dress, newly elected Patrick Henry proposed to the House of Burgesses his Resolves against the British Stamp Act. The debate next day was, as Thomas Jefferson observed, "most bloody."

"Tarquin and Caesar each had his Brutus," Henry thundered, "Charles the First his Cromwell, and George the Third —"

"Treason!" interrupted Speaker John Robinson, and others shouted "Treason! Treason!"

"— may profit by their example," Henry finished. "If this be treason, make the most of it!"

Jefferson observed later that Patrick Henry "certainly gave the first impulse to the ball of the revolution."

On May 15, 1776, however, when the fifth and most productive Virginia Convention met in Williamsburg, Henry hesitated to make the open break for freedom until America had allies against Great Britain.

The ball of the revolution passed to Edmund Pendleton, who presided as the Convention declared Virginia an independent Commonwealth and instructed Virginia delegates to the Second Continental Congress to propose American independence.

A few days later George Mason came to the fore (arriving for the session tardily as usual) and led in framing a State Constitution and presented a Declaration of Rights, which guaranteed to individuals the security of government by law. (Later James Madison incorporated Mason's Declaration in the United States Constitution's Bill of Rights.)

That was the Virginia way, one bold spirit after another seizing the initiative for the cause of freedom.

"We built a government slowly. I hope it will be founded upon a rock," Pendleton observed in a note to Jefferson.

But the patriots' sure, creative strokes came with dazzling rapidity.

"They seemed to have a feeling of urgency about the importance of doing a great deal now," Colonial historian Jane Carson has observed. "They all pushed, they all had the feeling that life is short and should be active."

Visitors to Williamsburg gradually sort out the Royal Governors. Save only Lord Dunmore, who had the misfortune to come along at the time of the Revolution, they were not a bad lot.

Sir William Gooch, for instance, fostered a sound system for grading and selling tobacco.

To Jefferson, Francis Fauquier was the ablest. At dinners in the Governor's Palace with the polished Fauquier, mathematics Professor William Small, and lawyer George Wythe, Jefferson heard, he remembered in old age, "more good sense, more rational and philosophical conversations, than in all my life besides."

That jolly party-giver, Lord Botetourt, so endeared himself to Virginians that when he died, they erected a statue to his memory. It stands in William and Mary's Earl Gregg Swem Library, and an inscription conveys his Lordship's benign outlook: "Let Wisdom and Justice preside in any Country, The People will rejoice and must be happy."

Governor Alexander Spotswood, left the most to restore. He had a hand in building the Wren Building, the Powder Magazine, Bruton Parish Church, and his own residence, which Virginians called the "Palace," first derisively because of its cost and then in pride for its elegance.

A long-faced, straight-lipped soldier, Spotswood commissioned two sloops that brought Blackbeard the pirate to bay in Ocracoke. In thousands of miles of travel, Spotswood's most fabled excursion was with the Knights of the Golden Horseshoe to the Blue Ridge. After parrying with stubborn Virginians 12 years, he ended by joining them as a planter near Fredericksburg. He loosed, it is said, skylarks on the Rappahannock.

In Colonial Virginia one Williamsburg resident failed to get along with any Royal Governor. Commissary James Blair, Rector of Bruton Parish Church and first president of William and Mary, was a one-man forerunner of the Revolution. The contentious Scotsman picked quarrels with three Governors and forced them out of office. Retiring beaten from bouts with Blair, Spotswood called him "that old Combustion."

The Commissary interested the planters in starting a college and journeyed to England to win the Crown's support. While waiting months for royal grants, he persuaded three pirates to try to win pardons by sharing their booty with the College.

In his 80s Blair was still a trial to good-natured Governor Gooch who thought it best "to kill him with kindness, but there is no perplexing device within his reach that he does not throw in my way. Unless he has all and does all, he is not satisfied; . . ."

Bruton Parish Church is a sturdy building of mellow red brick. The white-walled interior is softly austere. Sun streams through clear panes of tall windows that offer to the wandering eye a view of gray branches against the blue sky. One of America's oldest Episcopal churches, it fills each Sunday with members, tourists, college students,

Capitol of Colony flies Union Jack on spire above cupola

Under the fall foliage, Visitors leave the handsome, glowing, restored Capitol. It was the key building in the Colony. The House of Burgesses met in one of the great bay wings and the Council and the general court in the other. A gallery over an arcaded piazza connects the two bays and has a conference room in which councilors and burgesses settled their differences.

Mile-long Duke of Gloucester Street is heart of Williamsburg

Horses, liveried driver, and carriage wend their way slowly past dormers, shutters, and shop windows along the Duke of Gloucester Street. An artist bends over her pad to catch the subtle shades of colors on houses and shops. Along this street, after a Phi Beta Kappa banquet at the College of William and Mary, walked the Rev. W. A. R. Goodwin and John D. Rockefeller Jr. and plotted how they would restore the dilapidated town to its old Colonial glory. The work began in 1926. Town has 138 major buildings and gardens on 173 acres.

Williamsburg has more than 100 persons operating a score of crafts

A familiar landmark, the first the tourist sees from the bus, is Robertson's Wind-mill. A post mill, the earliest form known, the structure revolves atop a huge post of hewn timber. It could be hauled from place to place. The upper chamber holds the main shaft and millstones. Lower holds screening and sacking machinery. Householders visited mill twice a week. They could buy meal or flour with cash or bring

their own grain and allow the miller to exact his percentage for grinding it. In high wind the customers helped the miller furl the sails. Above, coopers trim staves in a shop where colonial craftsmen made tubs, buckets, barrels, and the huge tobacco hogshead.

Before the Robert Carter House is a tree, a paper mulberry, that catches the eyes of children with its frantic, frozen motion. It is a gnarled, grotesque and comical tree, all popping eyes, probing nose, and waving arms, importuning the passer-by to stay, a tree out of Mad Magazine by Gustav Doré. If the tree is faintly alarming, there is something eminently satisfying about the Public Magazine, the Powder Horn, standing in the southern half of Market Square. It is an octagonal building, with walls two feet thick, and a peaked roof. An encircling wall is 10 feet high. Governor Spotswood supervised its construction in 1715–16. On April 20, 1775, Governor Dunmore removed the powder stored in the Magazine. Patrick Henry, leading Hanover County Troops, forced payment of twice the powder's equivalent.

Sheep graze on the court-house green, under the eye of the Courthouse of 1770. Two courts met here, the James City County Court and the hustings or municipal court. The county court was a seat of power, both executive and judicial in Colonial Virginia. For years the "court-house boys," the officials and their friends, constituted the framework of politics throughout the Commonwealth of Virginia.

Williamsburg's varied panorama includes sheep, horses, and an apoplectic tree

Citizen soldiers — silversmith, blacksmith, cabinet maker, baker — fire flintlock muskets is a muster on market squa

...yday attire, brass buckle shoes to tricorn hat, members of the Colonial Williamsburg Militia Company protected capital.

Fifes and drums reverberate on Market Square, Duke of Gloucester Street

Freemen, 21 to 60, served in the local militia. Only a few, such as clergymen, were exempt. From early April through mid-October, the militia musters twice a week to demonstrate 18th century drills on the Market Square. In the muster above, the color guard bears Revolutionary flags. At right, massed fifers, drummers in bright red coats march down the Duke of Gloucester Street. The Capitol's spire is in the background. Each American unit had fifers and drummers to beat the duty calls, give commands on the battlefield and rally the scattered troops.

Church, Crown lift spires in contrasting style in old Williamsburg

Square tower and octagonal steeple soar above sturdy Bruton Parish, the oldest Episcopal church of uninterrupted use in the United States. Designed by Governor Spotswood, the church was completed in 1715. Graceful spire on reconstructed Governor's Palace looks down on the formal garden and ballroom wing. Spotswood also directed the building of the Palace. Completed in 1720, it served as residence for seven Royal Governors and for Patrick Henry and Thomas Jefferson, the first two Governors of the Commonwealth during the Revolutionary War period.

and even an occasional President of the United States.

In November, 1967, President Lyndon Johnson came to Williamsburg near the close of a continental tour of military bases. In Bruton, secure, he must have thought, from questions on the Vietnam War, the rangy, ruddy President threw his arm behind Mrs. Johnson's shoulders and let his head loll just a trifle.

But the Rev. Cotesworth Pinckney Lewis had been thinking, as he explained later, about what he could say that would strengthen the Chief Executive's heart and hand. In his sermon he reviewed aspects of the war troubling the Nation, and then said, "While pledging our loyalty, we ask humbly, WHY?"

The Rector's question evoked a mixed public response, but his catechizing Authority surely would have drawn the Commissary's approving nod.

The reconstructed Colonial Capitol, a "commodious pile" of pink brick, is built in the shape of an H: two bolster-like towers connected by a cross-bar of a gallery over an arcaded plaza.

(Lieutenant Governor Henry Howell chose to be inaugurated in 1971 between the two bolsters – and reported that the evening before, walking under the stars, he had heard George Mason urging, "Right on, fellow Virginian, right on!")

The House of Burgesses met in one wing of the Capitol, the Governor's Council in the other, and they composed their differences in joint committee rooms over the arcade. Mainly, they saw eye-to-eye. Many Councilors had served as burgesses, and members of both bodies were neighbors, friends, and often kin. Further, the leadership and the people had the same interests. What was good for the big planter was good for the little one – and the man who intended to become one in a country where land was cheap. The Capitol is a diagram of representative government in brick.

The stately Governor's Palace – two stories beneath a steep and many-dormered hip roof, topped by a lantern cupola rising between multiple chimneys – befitted a ruler whose domain extended to the Great Lakes and the Mississippi. Throughout are touches of elegance. In the ballroom ample enough for 200 guests, Governor Francis Fauquier held concerts with string pieces, woodwinds, and harpsichord. For at least once in his life, the hostesses note, Thomas Jefferson played second fiddle.

In the Palace's terraced formal gardens is a maze of holly trees with closely woven winding paths. Overlooking the maze is a double-terraced earth pyramid built to insulate the ice house. From the pyramid's top the visitor can look down on heads bobbing about, bewildered, in the maze, and hear an anxious mother calling: "You can come out aw-ready!"

Another delight is a pleached arbor of beeches arched over a frame to form a shady tunnel with portholes opening on bright gardens. A similar alley of hornbeam, a cool retreat, graces the rear of the Wythe House beside the Palace Green.

America's first law professor, George Wythe taught Jefferson, James Monroe, John Marshall, and Henry Clay. To Jefferson, Wythe was "my faithful and beloved mentor in youth and my most affectionate friend through life."

Virginia's first signer of the Declaration of Independence, Wythe was a generous, gentle man, "the Cato of his country," said Jefferson, "without the avarice of the Roman, for a more disinterested person never lived."

Chancellor of Virginia from 1778 to 1801, Wythe wrote an opinion in 1782 upholding the right of judicial review: ". . . if the whole legislature . . . should attempt to overleap the bounds . . . I, in administering the public justice of the country, will meet the united powers, at my seat in this tribunal; and, pointing to the constitution, will say, to them, here is the limit of

Words in the Hall of House of Burgesses were prelude to the victory at Yorktown

Costumed guide for Colonial Williamsburg gestures and speaks to tourists in the Hall of the House of Burgesses at the Capitol where Patrick Henry proposed his resolves against the British Stamp Act and cried his defiance of the King in his famed "Caesar-Brutus" speech. Such sentiments sparked the war, which ended, right, at Yorktown, where George Washington and French Admiral de Grasse joined their forces to defeat Cornwallis and the English. In the Hall, Virginians adopted a Constitution and Declaration of Rights.

55

your authority; and hither, shall you go, but no further!"

Wythe's great rival in court was Caroline County lawyer Edmund Pendleton, self-taught, practically self-made, but always willing to share his lore. Jefferson called him the ablest man he ever met in debate, "for if he lost the main battle, he returned upon you, and regained so much of it as to make it a drawn one, by dexterous maneuvers, skirmishes in detail, and the recovery of small advantages which, little singly, were important all together...."

Pendleton once taught George Washington a legislative lesson. When young Washington's bill "to prevent Hogs from running at large in the Town of Winchester" failed to pass, Pendleton assured its approval by retitling it "a Bill to Preserve the Water for the Use of the Inhabitants of the Town of Winchester ... by preventing Hogs from running at large."

Old, on crutches, Pendleton presided over the month-long Virginia Convention in Richmond that ratified, after bitter debate, the Nation's Constitution in 1788. Frequently he left the chair to defend the Constitution. Then, as the Convention closed, he brought friends and foes to tears with a plea: "We are brothers; we are Virginians. Our common object is the good of the country. Let our rivalry be who can serve his country with the greatest zeal; and the future will be fortunate and glorious."

To enjoy Colonial Williamsburg walk about and let the eye be surprised by odd angles of roofs; stroll among 90 acres of formal gardens and watch a mockingbird show white wing-patches, like a flirt flashing a fan; pause at a lagoon, covered in lily pads and white blooms and hear the sudden deep spunk of a bull frog; run a hand over the knots and whorls of a paper mulberry's massive trunk, frenzied motion frozen; discover a cherry tree curtseying over a white rail fence, its branches glistening with tiny red suns.

Amid swarming shoppers at the commercial end of the Duke of Gloucester Street strides a bespectacled youth, lean and tall as a rake, clad in green waistcoat, knee breeches, and high-collared shirt, on his way home after a day's duty as a costumed Colonial guide. Suddenly time slips a notch, the tourists are wraiths, and the youth is striding to a class with George Wythe, in the Wren Building.

"That the future may learn from the past" is Williamsburg's motto. Not long after the restoration began, former Governor Colgate Darden Jr. suggested a lesson to be learned. Although appreciative of the Rockefeller efforts, he said that the Commonwealth should have had the initiative and vision to save Williamsburg. Gas tax receipts alone from the increased tourist trade would have paid for the State's investment. Lulled into smug-ness by a great past, he said, Virginia too often has waited for others to do what it was well able to do. But other opportunities constantly arise, and Virginia can meet them, if it will.

History arranged it conveniently so that the American Revolution ended at Yorktown only a 15-minute drive on the National Parkway from Williamsburg where the Fifth Virginia Convention had called for independence. For George Washington and his soldiers the journey consumed seven years and thousands of miles and lives.

The battlefield 50 feet above the York River seems more fit for a picnic than a fight. Yorktown Historian Charles Hatch frequently directed tourists' attention to a bird perched in a cannon mouth – and then described the artillery moving in a cold rain, men swearing, shells bursting.

For Washington it was the last – and really, the first – chance to defeat the British. Nothing else in American history illustrates better than Yorktown the virtue of hanging on. Along the way Washington won an infrequent battle to boost troop morale and revive Congress, but mainly his mission had been to stay alive and not come in contact with the enemy – the Old Fox, the British called him.

In the Yorktown Information Center the visitor comes bang upon Washington's staff tent, pitched as it was in the field, and realizes that the patch of canvas sheltered America's main hope for victory. Washington's tent was the mobile headquarters for a new, often faltering nation.

In April 1781, a few months before the Yorktown campaign, Washington wrote to Lafayette: "We are at this hour suspended in the balance . . . our troops are fast approaching to Nakedness . . . our hospitals are without medicines and our sick without nutriment . . . our public works are at a Stand . . . But why need I run into detail, when it may be declared at a word, that we are at the end of our tether, and that now or never our deliverance must come."

Deliverance came suddenly. Cornwallis harried his way through the Carolinas and chased through Virginia after "that boy" Lafayette. Washington's army slipped away from the New York front, met the French forces, and dug in with 16,000 men before Yorktown where Cornwallis had 9,000. The move coincided beautifully with the arrival in Chesapeake Bay of Admiral de Grasse's French fleet from the West Indies. It cut off Cornwallis from help by sea. At Yorktown Washington brought it all together masterfully in October, 1781.

The siege's climax was the Allies' assault on two outlying redoubts. Lieutenant Colonel Alexander Hamilton led a bayonet charge that cleared Redoubt 10 in 10 minutes and the French stormed Redoubt 9 in half an hour. At his position near the front line, Washington said, "The work is done, and well done. Billy [his body servant] hand me my horse."

The Holy City

In 1609, 150 colonists, who had been sent from Jamestown to establish a fort at the Falls on the heights overlooking the James, built, instead, on the low ground near their boat. They called the area "World's End." Captain John Smith, when he came to inspect their work, showed his usual superior judgment. He bought from an Indian chief the high land and named it "None-Such," because, he said, there was "no place so strong, so pleasant and delightful." He planned to build there, but on returning from the trip to the Falls, he received the gunpowder wound that sidelined him in England. For him the home above the James remained a dream, None-Such.

Next to extol the site was William Byrd II. In September, 1732, while exploring his properties along the Roanoke and Dan Rivers, he reported in his journal that one evening when he and his party returned to camp, "we laid the foundation of two large cities. One at Shacco's to be called Richmond, and the other at the point of Appomattox River to be named Petersburg. These Major Mayo offered to lay out into lots without fee or reward. The truth of it is, these two places, being the uppermost landing of James and Appomattox Rivers, are naturally intended for marts where traffic of the outer inhabitants must center. Thus we did not build castles only, but also cities in the air."

Coming from the south, looking across the James River, the traveler today sees Richmond's skyline, an immense, wide-spreading tapestry hanging along the horizon. On a misty day the jumble of solid structures seems insubstantial, an airy mirage that the eye might blink away. Coming west, too, across Church Hill, the visitor has a noble prospect of spires, blocks, and towers – a variety of castles in the air that would stir the visionary, acquisitive Father Byrd. His Tory son, William Byrd III, trying to recoup a squandered fortune, auctioned off the lots for the town in 1768.

In other Virginia cities older residents sometimes refer to Richmond as the Holy City. Most Richmonders are oblivious to their city's having any such exalted station, although in addition to being, without much apparent exertion, the State's leading manufacturer, it also is the seat of the General Assembly. For four years it was the Capital of the Lost Cause, "the Troy of the War Between the States." To the American historian, said novelist Mary D. Johnston, "Richmond has the appearance an touch of cloth of gold." It also is "the Tobacco Capital of the World."

Richmonders are pleasantly aware of these distinctions, but of fundamental importance to them, the city simply always has been there and always will be, changing, true, but not at such a rate that there are not ample reminders of what it was yesterday. If, despite the natural advantages recognized by Father Byrd, it has not shot up like an Atlanta or even a Charlotte, and certainly not a Dallas, then it grows at its own sweet will, as surely as the gray lichens sheathing the oaks in Capitol Square or the flaming green patina streaking the great bronze statues along Monument Avenue. Richmond will get there by and by. Some conjecture that Washington, D.C.'s being 100 miles away stunts Richmond's expansion, but the explanation could simply be that Richmond does not want to boom. It wouldn't be Richmond if it did. If the rate of change accelerated markedly, Richmond wouldn't be able to accomodate the transition to its own pace. Ambitious invaders from other regions don't alter Richmond; like China, it assimilates and converts them. Its inhabitants are, for the most part, content with the city as a place, not just to get ahead, but, first and foremost, to live, with modern conveniences, yes, but also with the reassuring presence of certain familiar institutions and traditions, like old pieces of furniture, handed down through generations, comforting to the touch.

Richmond's towers overlook Shockoe Valley and tracks. At right, on Broad Street, City Hall raises its tall spire behir

/ *Hospital complex. At far left is Main Streets' financial district. Capitol's roof, left center, nestles amid masonry.*

The WRVA helicopter, hovering in the picture like God's spy, sees, along with the rush-hour traffic, a city of museums: the White House of the Confederacy, the attic of the Lost Cause, containing among other mementoes, a tattered flag carried by a North Carolina regiment through more than 50 engagements; the Valentine Museum, keeper of the city's past, where one may view the deep-cut features in the death mask of Stonewall Jackson, grim as Joshua, or gaze at the tiny boots (size: 4½-B) worn by General Robert E. Lee, and, departing, for a quarter, select an arrowhead from a heap of flints in a bowl by the door; Battle Abbey, the Valhalla of the South, with the Four Seasons of the Confederacy, billboard-sized murals of gray warriors, done by artist Charles Hoffbauer; and the Virginia Museum, where master showman Leslie Check Jr. beguiled an ordinarily thrifty General Assembly into flinging money into the fine arts, the first state-supported museum that launched the first artmobiles, museums on wheels, to carry ancient Egypt to Chilhowie.

The helicopter shepherding Richmonders to and from work also scours past old houses and buildings, beginning on Old Church Hill, the base from which the city spread, now renewed as home-hunting Richmonders find their way back. Anchoring the neighborhood on Broad Street is St. John's Church, where, during the Second Virginia Convention, Patrick Henry issued a call to arms, each point in his speech seeming to be the last possible peak, until he cried: "Give me liberty or give me death!"

It is pretty nearly the perfect oration, and one fellow, who had found a perch in an easterly window at St. John's, nearly facing Henry, asked not for liberty or death but simply to be buried on that spot, and was.

Henry's part in the Virginia debate of 1788 over the ratification of the United States Constitution occupied a fifth of the proceedings; but the finest portions were lost when the awe-struck official recorder laid down his pen to gape and listen and forgot to take notes. Henry didn't bother to revise his remarks in the journal; there'd always be another speech. His audience, aroused, and Henry, drained, didn't fret about posterity. It was all for now.

Henry, portraits show, had a long, pale face, spectacles pushed impatiently above his forehead; large, glowing eyes; a probing break of a nose, almost vulture-like, and a wide dip-mouth, curved and pointing downward at the middle, like gull's wings, that made the words fly.

Below Church Hill, on lower East Main Street, is Richmond's oldest dwelling, the Old Stone House, built in 1680 from unhewn river stone, also called the Po' How-us, not that it is a refuge for indigents but because it is the center of a four-building complex dedicated to Edgar Allan Poe, as well as to Richmond's early days.

The Poe Foundation has taken a place with which the poet had no visible connection and made it redolent of his brooding personality – a triumph of transference. Poe, who loved masks and mysteries, would revel in the atmosphere. The composed stone face that the house turns on busy Main Street conceals a loggia, a green-gleaming gem of a garden, and another house constructed from materials of dwellings in which Poe's foster mother lived, as artful a fabrication as one of Poe's tales of mystery and imagination. In the composite house, the visitor sees the desk where the poet wrote, his walking cane, and, from his childhood home with parents who had adopted him as a baby, a chair with a raven carved into the top – and perhaps into the child's imagination. Strolling through the rooms the visitor hears lines and titles still vivid from high school recitations and the croaking of the Raven with its famous, final Nevermore! – toward which, reciting the poem by rote before the class, one struggled as to a life preserver. Moralists shake their heads over Poe's drunkenness. The wonder is that amid poverty and tragedy he produced so much beauty. An underpaid editor of *The Southern Literary Messenger,* he scarcely had enough money to keep a roof over his child-bride's head; now the remnants of his tumultuous passage – a desk, a cane, a chair – are gathered in one of Richmond's most revered houses. Oh, Nevermore!

At Ninth and Marshall Streets is the sturdy brick home of John Marshall. To the rear rises the many-windowed Federal building, which the Chief Justice's opinions helped establish. What Marshall saw in the army during the Revolution – he fought at Brandywine, Germantown, Monmouth, and Stony Point and shared Valley Forge's hardships – convinced him of the necessity of a strong central government.

His portrait in the dining room of his home shows an arresting face: long-drawn, square-chinned, with deep-set dark and glowing eyes and firm, straight mouth. He was a man of thorough and quick resolve, who could relax and enjoy good companionship, as he did at home, reading aloud with his invalid wife, his dear Polly, and writing her, when they were parted, tender notes, love letters through a life-time. He also enjoyed the camaraderie at the Barbecue Club on Parson John Buchanan's farm, swapping yarns and tossing quoits, or horseshoes. As you pass 1000 West Clay Street it is pleasant to know that the Chief Justice of the United States threw horseshoes about here and got on his knees to measure a close one with a straw.

A rangy, loose-jointed, casually dressed frontiersman like his sandy-haired cousin in Monticello, he was equally as fearless as Jefferson in expounding views. It was a match of giant kinsmen when the two contended over the nature of the Union – Jefferson upholding the rights of the states, Marshall the Supreme Court's power to review legislation, both

Richmonders stroll along downtown Broad Street

Richmond's Broad Street begins where the city itself began, on old Church Hill, then runs through Shockoe Valley, climbs the hill past the Medical College of Virginia, and goes through the heart of the downtown shopping district, and on and on, passing used car lots, and wondrous shopping centers and suburbs. At last it becomes the highway to Charlottesville. Broad is a long street.

with an eye to safeguarding the individual, a check and a balance to each other.

The most dramatic confrontation of cousins occured during the trial of Aaron Burr in the State Capitol. While Jefferson raged at Monticello over the man who had threatened his Union, Marshall presided over the proceedings in the old Hall of the House of Delegates, dedicated to the law wherever it led, and a third cousin, erratic, brilliant John Randolph of Roanoke was chairman of the jury. A fourth, Edmund Randolph, former U.S. Attorney General, appeared as defense counsel.

Showing that Burr and his armed men never performed a treasonable act when they sailed down the Mississippi River, Edmund Randolph argued that no man should be tried for intentions, only his deeds. Chief Justice Marshall and the jury agreed, and the case ended with an acquittal – poetic justice for Randolph whose career had been ruined by a false charge of treason.

Marshall worked 34 years on the Court, until he was 80, and died on a trip to Philadelphia, surrounded by his tall sons who had hurried to his bedside. As the people bore his body through the streets to the dock to go home to Virginia, the Liberty Bell, ringing for John Marshall, cracked.

Just opposite Capitol Square at 707 East Franklin is the Norman Stewart House, the Civil War home of General and Mrs. Lee, the only residence in a block of shiny band-box office buildings. A four-story brick structure, it has a white, neo-classic porch at the northeast corner.

Familiar to most Virginians is the post-war photograph of Lee, the civilian, in a light gray suit, holding a low-crowned hat at his side, standing under the little portico at 707. So stamped is that image in memory that on a late afternoon, as sky-scrapers' shadows engulf the white portico, Virginians see him yet, the patient eyes turned courteously to a caller on the walk of herringbone brick. Lee on the porch of the prim narrow house is real; the shimmering buildings the mirage.

Rheumatic Mrs. Lee rested in a roller-chair on the rear veranda shaded by ailanthus trees. She looked south toward Petersburg where for 10 months her husband's tattered troop held the hammering armies of Ulyssee S. Grant.

She was – chattering, bright-eyed, sharp-chinned – a wren-like woman, busy making socks and gloves for the Confederacy. Soldiers, coming and going for meals or beds, called 707 "the Mess," and someone said that Mrs. Lee's daughters and friends sewing or folding bandages formed an industrial school.

Baskets of socks went to the hospitals in tobacco warehouses, where, the story went, once the soldiers put them on, they couldn't rest until they returned to duty. A man's feet had to march, they said, in "General Lee's socks."

His letters to her abound in grateful references to the warm gear for the men. On February 23, 1865,

61

acknowledging the arrival of a supply, he wrote, "you will have to send down your offerings as soon as you can, and bring your work to a close, for I think General Grant will move against us soon . . . no man can tell what may be the results . . ."

When General Lee abandoned Petersburg, Richmonders set fire to their own city. One excited citizen had to be dissuaded from blowing up alternate houses on the block to protect Lee's home. Next day a Richmond lady was indignant at seeing a Yankee guard pacing before 707, but presently the door opened, and the Federal soldier took a neatly arranged tray and sat on the steps to eat what Mrs. Lee had sent out to him.

After the surrender at Appomattox, General Lee rode Traveller to Richmond. Men, women, and children, his son Robert wrote, "crowded around him cheering and waving hats and handker-chiefs . . . more like the welcome to a conqueror than to a despised prisoner on parole. He raised his hat . . . and rode quietly to his home on Franklin Street, where my mother and sisters were anxiously awaiting him."

Linwood Holton, the first Republican to be Governor of Virginia in this century, relaxes among predecessors

At Governor Holton's elbow, on canvas, is Mills E. Godwin Jr., then, moving down the gallery, Albertis S. Harrison Jr., J. Lindsay Almond Jr., Thomas B. Stanley, and John S. Battle.
Depicted at right is more art, Jean Antoine Houdon's famous statue of George Washington.
When the General Assembly asked Jefferson's advice, he, with his usual good taste, picked Houdon, and insured his life, so he would come to America. Jefferson advised Washington to wear his military coat.

Preparing to leave 707, Lee tried to pay rent but John Stewart wrote that if the General insisted on regarding the gift as a debt, then "the payment must be in Confederate currency, for which alone it was rented to your son."

Once visible for miles, "Mr. Jefferson's square box" in Capitol Square now is ringed by state office buildings and banks. Nevertheless, there is drama in discovering the hidden, energizing core of the State amid the Square's trees and surrounding masonry.

Across from the entrance at the top of the Square is gray St. Paul's Church, where on an April Sunday, 1865, a courier strode down the aisle and delivered to Jefferson Davis word that General Lee no longer could defend Richmond from Grant's armies.

In St. Paul's, legend says, Lee was attending communion services after the war when a bent, shabby old Negro man shuffled to the front and knelt at the railing. In the shocked silence, the stately Lee arose, walked down the aisle, and knelt beside the old man to share the communion cup. More interesting than the fact that the tale is fable is that white Southerners, who would do anything Lee told them to do, have perpetuated it.

Behind Capitol Square crouches the old City Hall, which many Richmonders regard as an eyesore and the more discerning as an encrusted gem. Only 41 per cent of its space is usable statisticians complain. But persons today too seldom have the experience of walking into a building and looking up four stories to a skylight in a loft large enough to house a blimp. A grand stairway, wide as a two-lane road, is set at what looks to be a 45-degree angle, fit for Cinderella's entrance. Iron pillars studding the interior are embellished with warts the size of golf balls. Despite carping critics, the toad in stone probably is safe, primarily because to destroy it would cost more than the price of a new building. The walls at the base are three feet thick.

Across Broad Street is the new City Hall, soaring 22 stories. Its observation deck offers an excellent view of Richmond, including the Richmond Coliseum, which resembles an old-timey top that sang as it spun, a intriguing, handsome building, its weathered, brown metallic exterior a refreshing contrast to so many cement-white public facades these days.

In the center of the Capitol building is the Rotunda. If the all-seeing eye of the helicopter could peer through the skylight at the top, as into the scenic interior of a sugared Easter Egg, it would find the Commonwealth's most prized art object, Jean Antoine Houdon's lifesized statue of George Washington, standing between the House of Delegates and the State Senate. The man it represents is central, too, in the Virginia ideal.

In 1784 the General Assembly voted to commission a statue of the General "to be of the finest marble and best workmanship" and turned trustingly to Jefferson, as Virginians did in such matters, to choose a sculptor. Jefferson, then in France, picked Houdon.

Washington was in his prime, about 53, four years away from the Presidency. He was reluctant to pose in a toga, and, fortunately for posterity, Jefferson agreed, and so the General put on his old military coat, with two buttons missing from one side and one from the other.

Houdon arrived in Mount Vernon in October, 1785. He had difficulty achieving just the right expression of firmness on Washington's face. And then one day, watching the Father of Our Country dickering with a trader over the price of a yoke of oxen, the artist saw the look of "majestic calm" he had been seeking and hurried away to his work to catch it on the model.

Sculptor Houdon had envisioned the life-sized likeness, depicting all 6'2" of Washington, standing amid his people; but James Madison wrote an inscription that raised the pedestal five feet. It would take too long for the General Assembly to authorize a short inscription, Houdon was informed. Anyway, Virginians were accustomed to looking up to Washington.

In niches around the Rotunda are marble busts of the other seven Virginia-born Presidents and of Lafayette. The General Assembly voted funds for Lafayette's bust in 1784 "as a lasting monument of his merit and their gratitude."

In the Depression's depths, 150 years later, Virginia got around to dedicating the busts, thanks to Governor John Garland Pollard (1930–1934). "He made the biggest to-do about those busts of distinguished Virginians that he unveiled around the Capitol," remembered Mrs. Pollard, his wife, who was secretary to four successive Governors. "But he was telling the people: 'You think we have hard times; look what these men did.'"

On the Capitol's third floor above Houdon's Washington is the Governor's office, the most prestigious State post in Virginia.

When the Governor steps out of his office, he is ringed by portraits of a dozen or so of his predecessors in a perpetual reception.

The Virginia Governor has been one of the strongest state executives in the Nation ever since 1928 when Governor Harry F. Byrd reorganized State government. The Governor is responsible for making the State budget and presenting it to the General Assembly. Through it, he shapes State policy. For instance, Governor Linwood Holton (1970–1974) attained through the budget a Cabinet of Secretaries.

Such has been the integrity of the occupants of the office that all a Governor carries with him when he leaves is the high-backed leather chair from which he served the Commonwealth for four years.

Visiting school children like to perch in the high-backed chair at the Governor's desk and feel for a moment that the Commonwealth is at their beck.

One time, Governor J. Lindsay Almond Jr. (1958 to 1962) remembered, some 75 children from a rural school climbed one after another in the chair. Then, just as they were leaving, one asked for the Governor's autograph, and the line formed again. The last boy seemed bashful, but when he observed the Governor's fast scrawl, he shouted: "Doggone! He don't write no better than I do!"

Another story shows how Virginians regard the office, as well as the homespun courtliness of Governor Thomas B. Stanley (1954–1958).

During Queen Elizabeth II's visit to Virginia in 1957, Governor Stanley showed her around the Capitol. When they entered his office, he, mindful possibly of the school children's custom, dutifully asked his royal guest if she would care to sit in the Governor's chair.

With so much power a Governor can, if he pleases, stay busy. When people asked William M. Tuck if he enjoyed being Governor (1946–1950), that mountainous man replied that he felt like the

Elk at Maymont Park has fans, but Pan plays music heard by none

On a summer Sunday in Richmond when the late sun turns the green hills gold above the James, a good place to be is Maymont Park. There are gardens, walkways, a wildlife exhibit, and the tan Victorian castle of Major James Dooley and his wife Sallie. They gave the park to Richmond, and a library as well. A Confederate veteran and a shrewd businessman, Major Dooley parlayed railroads, real estate, and mines into a Xanadu for Richmonders to enjoy.

Negro in the spiritual: "I'm in heaven, but I can't sit down."

"I had everything, but I was BUSY all the time. There was hardly a minute that I wasn't trying to solve something that was already happening or trying to avoid something that was about to happen.

"But once in a great while, just to keep from going crazy, I would slide away from the Mansion for 12 or 14 hours, go to my cabin, and sit around there and have a drink and pinch myself and think, 'Here I am up here. Hell, I don't reckon I'm Governor.' But then they'd be sending State police out there wanting to know where I was and asking what to do about this or that, and I'd think, 'Just might as well go back.'"

"About a week before my inauguration I saw Colgate Darden marching across the Square. He had on that Homburg hat and he was just a-whistling, the blithest thing I ever saw, and I said to myself: 'Goodness gracious, a man leaving the greatest office in the Commonwealth oughtn't to be that

happy.' Then when I took the oath, you could have heard him laugh for two miles. He just laughed and hollered, he was so relieved."

One of the Governor's tasks is to shape public opinion, and prepare the people for the fact that they must pay for what they demand. Governor Tuck sponsored a major tax increase to improve mental hospitals.

"What brought it on, the newspapers kept printing blown-up pictures of poor, unfortunate creatures in the disturbed wards and talking about the awful, awful conditions . . . and they were bad sure enough, and so we introduced the bill for funds to help, and then the newspapers that had demanded all these things fought the hell out of me. But we won."

The Governor told the people that the episode reminded him of an old tavern in the Northern Neck that had a room infested with ghosts. No guests could stay there. But finally a stranger was assigned to the room and spent the night.

Old St. John's, Robert E. Lee survey their neighborhoods in Richmond

In Old St. John's, a simple white frame church on East Broad Street, the Second Virginia Convention met and heard Patrick Henry ask for liberty or death. St. John's is the center of a revival as Richmond residents are returning to restore old homes on Church Hill where Richmond began. And at Monument and Allen, Robert E. Lee in bronze rides Traveller eternally and bareheaded, too, because sculptor Jean Antoine Mercie found "the brow of Lee too noble to be hidden under a hat."

Next morning the curious tavern keeper asked the guest if anything untoward had happened.

"Oh," he said, "I saw a few ghosts."

"What'd you do?"

"Well," he said, "we sang a while, we prayed a while, we preached a while."

"How'd you get rid of 'em?" asked the tavern keeper.

"Why," he said, "I got out the collection plate, and they all vanished!"

Fortunately, a Governor can call on a former Governor for help. When ex-Governor Tuck returned to the Capitol one day in 1964 to view changes underway in the historic structure, he darted into the Governor's inner office, pulled open the bottom drawer of the big desk, and peered inside. When he was inaugurated Governor in 1945, Tuck explained, he wrote Colgate Darden's telephone number inside the drawer for handy reference in times of crisis.

Others called on Darden, who is as close to being a Jefferson as is any Virginian this century. In 1963 Governor Albertis Harrison (1962–1966) asked him to stop by his office for a chat. As former Governor Darden recalled their interview, "Albertis said, with a perfectly straight face, 'There's a little something I want you to do for me. I want you to open the schools of Prince Edward County.'"

Governor Harrison scarcely could have delegated a more difficult task. When the United States Supreme Court ordered Prince Edward County to desegregate its public schools in May 1959, the Board of Supervisors declined to appropriate funds for education. The schools stayed closed four years.

"I can't go anywhere and make a speech," Harrison confided to Darden, "without somebody jumping up and asking what I'm going to do about the schools in Prince Edward."

Governor Harrison was just as casual about his request, Darden remembered, as if it was a little assignment that could be handled over a telephone.

"Fine," said Darden, "and is there any other little thing I can do for you while I'm about it?"

"No," said Governor Harrison, "that'll be enough for now."

So former Governor Darden headed the Prince Edward Free School Foundation that, backed mainly with private funds, opened the schools with a first-class teaching force. A year later the County resumed its financial support.

In 1968 Governor Mills Godwin (1966–1970) appointed former Governors Darden and Harrison to the 11-member commission offering revisions to the Virginia Constitution. At the Commission's urging, the General Assembly wrote education into the Virginia Bill of Rights. It also empowered the Attorney General to hold accountable any locality that failed to appropriate its share of education funds. The Assemblymen fixed, once and for all, the responsibility for support of the public schools.

Everybody has a Governor, remarked Governor Holton during his term, "and my Governor is Governor Darden." The fact that Holton was Virginia's first Republican Governor since Reconstruction did not deter him from asking Democrat Darden's advice. (He was especially heartened by Darden's support of his calm handling of a perplexing situation over the busing of school children.)

The Republican Governor and the Democratic General Assembly worked harmoniously. "I don't ask them to support my program but to do what they think best for the Commonwealth and not be bound by traditional ties," observed Holton. In turn he tended to be nonpartisan in major appointments.

By 1970 the Republicans had taken a fourth of the General Assembly's seats, but their party never stood taller than in the mid-1950s when they had only three State Senators, and one was Ted Dalton. In 1953, running for Governor, Senator Dalton hit every issue straight and true, and in 1957, campaigning again, he cried out against proposals to escape desegregation by closing schools.

Politics tends to be of high caliber in Virginia, with notes of grace that touch the public. In 1969 Holton defeated Democrat William C. Battle, who already had gone through a gruelling Democratic primary, plus a hectic runoff with Henry Howell. On election night, a happy Holton was telling a cheering throng in the Hotel John Marshall that he was "completely speechless," and was adding that "I want to express to Mr. Battle, who is a friend of mine —" when suddenly he was speechless at the sight of the man he had defeated pushing through the crowd with Mrs. Battle at his side.

The word — "Battle's here! Battle's here!" — spread through the packed hall. Hanging onto Battle, as to a life preserver, was Republican State Chairman Sam Carpenter of Arlington, babbling, "This is Virginia, dammit! This is Virginia!" — as an explanation of a just defeated loser coming directly to congratulate the winner. Then Battle's calm Indian profile was looking down at Holton, whose eyes and mouth were mere lines as he tried to contain his emotion, and the loser was raising the winner's hand, and saying, "All the best, old boy!"

As the Democrat made his way back through the celebrating sea of Republicans, a newsman said, "That was a fine thing to do!"

"That was the only thing to do," said Battle.

Virginia's problems are those of other states, but the people are patient, trusting, and forgiving. Most of all, the Governor knows that in a crisis he can rely on their good sense.

In Virginia a one-term Governor is never a has-been. When Governors gather on state occasions, a half-dozen with their gray heads together like nodding elephants, each is hailed with respect and affection. The Virginia people remember only the good.

The General Assembly is the oldest continuous legislative body in the Western Hemisphere, a mouthful to be sure, and one that some members enjoy proclaiming. It is, moreover — and this is its glory — an unusually honest body of public servants. In that high degree of integrity it reflects the Virginia government with thousands of State employes who give efficient, fair, impartial service. The Virginia people will put up with almost anything in their representatives except dishonesty and discourtesy.

The General Assembly is a reflective, as well as a legislative, body. The first action of the first Assembly in 1619 was to appoint a committee to study what to do next. Its descendants have honored that tradition. Indeed, for about two-thirds of the 20th Century, the General Assembly moved much like the jellyfish. It pulsated, advancing, then pausing. When it was holding regular sessions every two years, a Governor tried to push through as much of his program as possible in the first session because during the second half the General Assembly would be inclined to ruminate over what it had done. In 1966 the pace picked up and steadied.

For nearly a century the General Assembly was under the spell of the oldest continuous political machine in the Western hemisphere — the conservative Democratic Organization, founded by U.S. Senator Thomas Martin, refined by Harry F. Byrd.

Such devices as the poll tax helped confine the electorate to the elect, but they do not explain entirely the Organization's long tenure. Paradoxically, it maintained its hold by being forced to relax its grip periodically, giving a little with the times, enlivening the conservative sound doctrine with doses of progress from the platforms of those it defeated. Its opponents — Andrew Montague, Westmoreland Davids, Frances Pickens Miller, Robert Whitehead, Ted Dalton, Armistead Boothe — contributed to its longevity with their ideas.

Finally, the Organization's redeeming trait during Byrd's long day was its insistence on integrity in government. No one could raise the shout — Throw the rascals out! — that felled political machines elsewhere. In the end, the Organization declined through plain old age, hardening of political arteries. It forgot the lesson of its youth — to admit youth to power.

The Virginia people's instinct, inherited from the English, is to reconcile extremes. A broad electorate of both races and all economic segments offers an accurate reflection of the population, which always will have a broad conservative base.

The helicopter monitors rush-hour traffic over four east-west arteries: Main, Franklin, Grace and Broad Streets. At One West Main is a prim gray mansion, the home of Ellen Glasgow, the Queen of Virginia Letters. Nearby on Franklin is the handsome Richmond Public Library on the site of the childhood home of James Branch Cabell, the King. A rarity who lifted his Mephistophelian eyebrows

Historic houses of Marshall, Poe, and Lee enrich streets in Richmond

On East Main Street (upper right) is the oldest house in Richmond, and, further, one of the most imaginative, being a shrine to Edgar Allan Poe. Below the Poe House is the home of Chief Justice John Marshall who loved to play horseshoes and render a verdict on a close one with a straw. Finally, above, stands the war-time home of Robert E. Lee on 707 East Franklin Street.

at the world, he liked to say that he was born in the rare book room.

The two writers had an interesting love-hate relationship with each other and the city they celebrated. Somehow the critics have confused their literary identities. Urged by a publisher to write of optimism and the West, Ellen Glasgow replied bleakly that she knew as little about one as the other. But her portrayal of the Virginia scene is deeply tinged with the romantic, novelist-critic Louis Rubin Jr. has observed. No matter how barren the ground becomes for her Virginians, she manages usually to end on a note of optimism.

In his book *No Place on Earth* Dr. Rubin finds that Cabell novels, although set in mythological country, have an essential concern for the here and now. Once his characters arrive in Poictesme, existence in that never-never land is under the humdrum conditions of real life. The escape with which Cabell has so often been charged is a device to disclose that there is no escape.

Broad and Grace are the chief mercantile streets bounding two block-square department stores, to which, it is said, all good North Carolinians pass when they go to heaven. Just where Broad Street starts to dip into Shockoe Valley towers the Medical College of Virginia Hospital's original, cross-shaped structure built with Federal funds, as was the State Library across the way. Governor James Price (1938–1942) saw to that.

Richmonders claim that Monument Avenue is the longest straight street in the world. Certainly the tree-shaded thoroughfare is the most statue-studded.

Robert E. Lee's statue was the first they raised on Monument Avenue, atop a 40-foot granite pedestal in the center of a circular grass plot. There's room to stand back and look up at the lichen-green likeness of the man on the striding horse.

No other loser has been so idolized. When the soldiers went home, they added to the already widening legend, and the dignified, bearded Lee became mixed in the minds of their offspring with the deity.

When Lee died in October, 1870, the South, struggling still to pull to its feet, set about to raise funds for the statue.

In 1886 various memorial associations commissioned French sculptor Jean Antoine Mercie to do the work. On October 27, 1887, South Carolina's Wade Hampton, Lee's cavalry leader at the close, led the parade for the laying of the cornerstone. On May 4, 1890, the statue's bronze parts, weighing more than 12 tons, reached Richmond. May 7 was the date for transferring the parts from railroad-flat cars to four wagons. Veterans from the Lee and Pickett camps had expected to haul the wagons by hand, but boys arrived first, and so the veterans marched ahead along First Street to Franklin Street, where extra ropes were attached so the young and old might take hold. Spectators lined porches and windows of homes, and the veterans pulled at the ropes, and amid the cheers, suddenly faint and insubstantial, they thought of the long pull through four years of war, and that time was gone and this time was not real and only the sweat on their brows in the Virginia spring was tangible, and they brushed it away gratefully with their sleeves as they pulled the ropes, as evidence that they were there for one last common effort.

The unveiling took place May 29. The parade down Franklin featured tall John B. Gordon, who had led the last charge at Appomattox, and courteous Joseph Johnston, whose wounds were a history of the war, and stolid James Longstreet, who, when the feisty Federal, George Custer, demanded his surrender before negotiations at Appomattox, had risen, glaring, in his stirrups and offered to begin it all over again, dispatching orders to divisions long vanished.

Presiding at the unveiling was profane Jubal Early. As he watched the bobbing shoulders of the marching veterans, old Jube's eyes must have glistened, not in sentiment but in the wish that they had been at hand during the last long winter when he was trying to hold the Valley against increasing hordes of Yankees, his own forces dwindling finally, literally, to himself and a few aides. There had been a Sunday when Early and his staff listened to a preacher crying, "Suppose, my Christian friends, that those who have laid for centuries in their graves should arise now and come forth from their quiet resting places; and marching in their white shrouds should pass before this congregation, by thousands and tens of thousands, what would be the result?"

And Jube, leaning to the aide at his side, snarled, "I'd conscript every damn one of them!"

General Johnston, with a one-armed veteran on one side and a one-legged veteran on the other, looked out on the upturned faces and then turned and amid sudden hush, pulled the rope attached to the huge, hooded object on the pedestal, and the veil fell away and Lee came clear, riding serenely, gazing South.

Cannon thundered, muskets crashed, bands blared, the crowd roared. If the General, Mrs. Lee wrote, "had succeeded in gaining by his sword all the South expected and hoped for he could not have been more honored and lamented."

On Lee's flank at Monument and Lombardy is the equestrian statue to J.E.B. Stuart, plumed, and riding, half-turned in the saddle, looking back, as if, straining to thrust his horsemen between Richmond and Phil Sheridan's Yankees, he is calling, "Come on! Come on! They're just ahead!" A come-on, not a go-on, commander, his men called him.

At Monument and Belmont is a colonnade in stone to the memory of Jefferson Davis. He stands in frock coat at the foot of a soaring column, which is topped by a robed female pointing heaven-ward.

In 1907 the monument cost $70,000—$20,000 more than the General Assembly had appropriated the previous year in creating a state system of high schools. The City Planning Commission would like to re-erect it somewhere else. The statue was designed to mark an end to Monument Avenue, the planners argue, but the street kept lengthening, and now the motorist driving east to work sees the rear of the statuary and those racing west at sunset catch only a glimpse of Davis standing, right hand extended, as if feeling for rain.

What troubles planners is that the cement crescent reduces three lanes on each side to two. If motorists do not pause to read and reflect, they are aware intensely of Jefferson Davis as a bottleneck — as, indeed, he was regarded by some of his contemporaries. Which was unfair. Head of a new and sudden government, all Davis had in abundance was advice.

One other, likely, could have appreciated the task. Lincoln. After Richmond fell and Davis fled, Lincoln came up the James in a boat with Admiral David Porter. "Thank God, I have lived to see this day," Lincoln said. "It seems to me that I have been dreaming in a horrid dream for four years, and now the nightmare is gone. I want to see Richmond."

Lincoln walked up Richmond's hills, holding his son Tad by the hand, escorted by several sailors through a crowd of adoring blacks and past an occasional white face at a doorway or window. During the walk General Weitzel asked what he should do about the captive Richmonders. "I don't want to give you an order on that, General," Lincoln said, "but if I were in your place, I'd let 'em up easy. Let 'em up easy."

At 12th and Clay street Lincoln entered the White House of the Confederacy and inspected his adversary's quarters — it was history now, fast-receding — and he walked the rooms curiously, as if already the scene were another era. In the high-ceilinged office he sat in the chair at the desk and said, dreamily, "Now I am sitting in the chair from which Jefferson Davis ruled the South."

In going to the chair, Lincoln was like nearly every Union soldier who entered the room. Some dragged the chair out on the veranda so that a photographer might record that they had sat there. Indeed, today's visitor has an impulse, seeing it in the far corner, to step past the velvet guard-rope and sit in the chair where Davis and Lincoln sat.

Next in the parade of statues is the bronze likeness of Stonewall Jackson, a silent sentinel on Old Sorrel, facing north at Monument and Boulevard. A block beyond is the seated figure of Matthew Fontaine Maury, head bowed, a globe suspended above his shoulders, seeming to ponder the course of the Gulf Stream that he traced, and his own course, out of the Union and into the Confederacy where he turned his scientific genius to manufacturing mines, and into exile for a time after the war.

White House of Confederacy overlooks formal garden

70

Inside the White House of the Confederacy, a museum, the history-mind-d may see the sword that General Robert E. Lee wore he would never draw except in the defense of his native state and dour General Stonewall Jackson's sword and beatup cap, and Jeb Stuart's white plume, sadly bedraggled by the years. The history buff also may see the Great Seal and measure the meagre fistful of parched corn on which a soldier had to exist in the closing days of the dying Confederacy.

The hovering helicopter spies, along with museums and monuments, parks and colleges. South on the Boulevard from Jackson's statue is Byrd Park, and, adjoining it, Maymont Park, a legacy from Major James Dooley and his wife, Sallie May. A maimed hand from a wound at the Battle of Williamsburg did not deter the Major from amassing railroads, steel mills, and real estate after Appomattox. The Dooleys' turreted mansion of tan limestone and sandstone overlooks the James. Their estate's 100 acres contain Japanese and Italian gardens, marble statues of Greek deities in Victorian attitudes, and a wildlife exhibit donated by William Thalhimer Sr. and featuring elk, fuzzy antlered, and buffalo, long-bearded as if bees clustered at their lips for wisdom. The Dooleys, to their sorrow, were childless. Now their green and sunlit domain is aswarm with children.

Richmond is the home of three institutions of higher education, and close by, at Ashland, is a fourth, spirited Randolph-Macon College, the first founded in the United States by the Methodist Episcopal Church. (The church was induced to come to Ashland through a donation of land by the Richmond Fredericksburg & Potomac Railroad. The Methodists go right on singing hymns and founding colleges. Their most recent in Virginia is Virginia Wesleyan, in Norfolk.)

On Franklin Street in Richmond is Virginia Commonwealth University. It grew out of the Richmond Professional Institute that was born in 1917 when the Army sent an iron-jawed little man from Camp Lee to Richmond to train public health nurses through "the Richmond School of Social Work and Public Health," funded by several generous Richmonders. There, in an acorn, is VCU's family tree.

The founding father, Dr. Henry H. Hibbs, a Kentuckian with a doctorate from Columbia University, arrived at a school that had $500 and one teacher, himself. He and a few students met in two rooms over the old juvenile and domestic relations court on Capitol Street.

Undaunted, Dr. Hibbs went about during the Depression, buying rambling Victorian mansions on Franklin, Park, and Shafer Streets and paying the bills by renting them to students and teachers. He would entertain any idea for a valid course that would attract enough students to pay the teacher. Thus, he expanded the offerings as he had assembled the buildings. By the time the State awaked, he had acquired 20 properties, and Virginia had a growing school on its hands.

In 1952 the General Assembly resolved to investigate RPI's growth. The students protested, but Dr. Hibbs shushed them, explaining, cheerily, that "to get more money we have to become better known, and this may be the very way."

The proposed study never materialized. And when Virginia began to expand higher education to do its duty by college-age youth, RPI was ready for transformation into an urban university. (Under the guidance of Presidents Lewis Webb and James Bugg, William and Mary's Norfolk Division also thrust like a beanstalk past restraints into Old Dominion University for bustling Hampton Roads. Similarly, Norfolk State College won independence with President Lyman Brooks from its parent, Virginia State College in Petersburg. Meanwhile, in Northern Virginia, George Mason College separated from the University of Virginia. Thus, at mid-century, metropolitan centers of learning began developing along Virginia's thickly populated urban corridor from Washington, D.C. to Norfolk.)

Several blocks east of VCU is Virginia Union University founded by Northern Baptists in 1867 to educate former slaves. They leased on Broad Street what had been a slave trader's lockup – "Lumpkin's Jail" – for blacks who had rebelled at being sold south. The Baptists turned the cells into classrooms and made the whipping post a lectern. Along the way to its campus on Belvidere Street, Virginia Union absorbed three other schools.

In 1972 Mr. and Mrs. Sidney Lewis gave Virginia Union $2 million to launch a 10-year campaign for $18 million.

The Lewises told Virginia Union President Allix James that they had been blessed with good fortune and they intended to enjoy sharing it with others. (That year they also gave $9 million to Washington and Lee University and $2 million to the Eastern Virginia Medical School in Norfolk.) Meanwhile, the Ford Foundation included Virginia Union and Hampton Institute among eight first-line predominantly black colleges to receive up to $5 million annually for five years.

Among Virginia Union's alumni is Richmond-born author Robert Deane Pharr. *The Book of Numbers,* his raucous, tender novel about the numbers racket, conveys more compellingly than does a shelf of sociological treatises the reality of Southern cities' black communities during the 1930s. In other equally powerful novels he extends into the last quarter of the 20th century a panorama as revealing of black society as Ellen Glasgow's portrait of the white.

The white man's moment of truth, he writes, "is a pale and ignorant vanity that amuses all black men. It is a conceit, a game of mirror-mirror-on-the-wall, a childish fantasy. No American Negro has ever felt the need to climb a mountain or fight a bull; why should he yell at the waves in the ocean of fates?"

His work challenges blacks as well as whites. In *The Book of Numbers,* a character says fiercely, "Never ask me to condone the Negro's ignorance. I will do all in my power to eradicate it, but please do not ask me to forgive it. And besides ignorance needs no champions. It is a powerful thing that can crush truth to the ground without a whisper."

In soft, precise voice, he explained to a newsman his Richmond origins:

"My grandmother and grandfather were very proud of being Richmonders. In fact, my grandfather was the first black selectman from Jackson Ward, and my mother married my father who was a Union student, a preacher, whose first church was in Ann Arbor, Michigan. My older brother and sister were born there, and when it was time for me to be born, my grandmother wrote my mother and said, 'You should have at least one of your children born on Virginia soil.' And so my mother came here so I could be born."

Another Baptist-backed institution, the University of Richmond, received a dramatic assist toward excellence. At the annual trustees meeting in 1967, President George M. Modlin talked candidly about the University's two choices: (1) continue to do its best with limited resources and suffer a gradual weakening or (2) grow in quality through a contribution of—and here Dr. Modlin wrote on the blackboard $25,000,000 to $50,000,000 — from some benefactor. The more trustee E. Claiborne

Robins reflected, the more he through that $25 million was not enough. "If it was worth doing at all, it had to be done right," he said. Further, it would be better, rather than make the gift a bequest, "to do it now and watch the progress." In 1969 he gave the $50 million.

In his youth he rode the Westhampton streetcar to and from college, shelved books at night in the Richmond Public Library, and coached classmates in languages. He had no time for campus activities, but, he recalled, smiling, "I probably wouldn't have participated anyway. I was shy, awfully shy."

His father had died when the boy was two years old. While the youth worked his way through the Medical College of Virginia Pharmacy School, his mother held together the apothecary shop.

"My father really had just begun the business when he died at 39," he said. "I couldn't let her down after she had held it together more than 20 years."

After graduation with honors, he borrowed $2,000, and he, his mother and a Negro employe mixed the drugs which he took on the road to sell through North Carolina. That was the start of the multimillion dollar A.H. Robins Co., and E. Claiborne Robins has held to the habit of hard work and the sense of loyalty with which he began.

Those traits also characterized the University's most consistent benefactors, the faculty members. For years they worked for meager pay as, indeed, did the teachers in Virginia's other hard-strapped independent colleges.

But they did not stint of themselves in teaching. They spread a bounty before their students. And the University never wavered in supporting their right to teach as they believed.

A fiery, inspiring history professor, Dr. S. C. Mitchell, used to greet freshmen by thundering: "Your fathers learned the great secret: It's sweet to live by the sweat of another man's brow!"

Perhaps President Frederick W. Boatwright's greatest hour occurred during a financial campaign that failed. In 1936 the University was seeking $500,000. Exploding at the campaign's start was a charge by some businessmen that Dr. Mitchell was teaching social and economic heresies.

Then Dr. Boatwright made his reply. "We must encourage our teachers and students to think," he said, "and we should not be surprised when they do not think alike. The inquiring mind will question established custom in every field of human action...

"While I believe the teacher in a Christian college should have a decent respect for current public opinion, it is nevertheless true that a college is more concerned with teaching students how to think than with telling them what to think...

"Is not reasonable freedom to think and speak worth too much in these times and in this section of our country for men of wealth to try to bludgeon this freedom into silence by depriving the university of needed financial support?"

Thomas Jefferson's way

Looking at Monticello, we feel that the tall master of the house himself might step forth at any moment, come out to greet Lafayette on his Farewell Tour or to organize his grandchildren for a race, taking care that the youngest have a headstart. No home more clearly bespeaks the builder than does Monticello. One never tires of visiting the house because, like its creator, it always is revealing a new facet. Thomas Jefferson and Monticello are inexhaustable.

When other planters were placing their homes along river banks near their wharfs and crops, Jefferson set a mansion on a mountain. To the west was his beloved Blue Ridge. Below was the village of Charlottesville. To the east was his "sea view" of farms stretching away through the Piedmont.

Where, he inquired, "has nature spread so rich a mantel under the eye? mountains, forests, rocks, rivers. With what majesty do we there ride above the storm! How sublime to look down into the workhouse of nature, to see her clouds, hail, snow, rain, thunder, all fabricated at our feet! and the glorious sun, when rising as if out of a distant water, just gilding the tops of the mountains, and giving life to all nature."

In 1782, the Chevalier de Chastellux, one of Rochambeau's Generals, visited Jefferson and found him "the first American who has consulted the fine arts to know how he should shelter himself from the weather." It seemed to Chastellux as if Jefferson from his youth "had placed his mind as he had done his house, on an elevated situation, from which he might contemplate the universe."

Jefferson tended his gardens and terraced and planted the little mountain until it was like a hanging basket of flowers and trees. "No occupation is so delightful to me as the culture of the earth, and no culture comparable to that of the garden," he wrote in 1811. "Such a variety of subjects, some one always coming to perfection, the failure of one thing repaired by the success of another, and instead of one harvest a continued one through the year. Under a total want of demand except for our family table, I am still devoted to the garden. But though an old man, I am but a young gardener."

Finally there is superbly proportioned Monticello, dark-red brick walls contrasting with the matching snow white porticoes supported by slender columns and capped by the octagonal white crown. The visitor is not as aware of Monticello's mass as he is that of the river plantations' cliff-like facades. Indeed, by concealing dependencies below terraces, setting back a half story, and lengthening windows to cover a story and a half, Jefferson minimized Monticello's bulk that contains 35 rooms. The exquisite design draws the eye from one feature to another so that the whole *is* greater than the sum of its parts. Jefferson worked on his house lovingly for 39 years. It was he.

Inside are his innovative gadgets. The ordinary tourist, the male, anyway, does not know a hepplewhite from a chippendale. His eyes glaze, his knees buckle at the sight of one more chair, which he would rather sit upon than study. What a relief to enter Monticello and come upon the results of Jefferson's tinkering: the shelves on revolving doors that turned between kitchen and dining room; a single, quartet-stand for musicians; the dumbwaiter, probably America's first, that conveyed wine from the cellar; his bed in an alcove so that he could, as he pleased, move into bedroom or his library with 6,500 volumes, and an aid, furthermore, in making the bed; the modest, concealed, space-saving stairways rather than the customary grand staircase; storm windows and folding doors; a replica of the portable desk he designed and on which he wrote the Declaration of Independence; the wondrous seven-day clock strung over the main entrance that tells the day of the week by descending Revolutionary War cannonballs; and, finally, the duplicating writing machine for a man who wrote 10 to 12 letters daily—the

Jefferson's lovely 'Monticello' caps mountain

Monticello's white dome looks out on piedmont farms, Charlottesville, and Blue Ridge Mountains. Set on broad lawns, amid green trees, the red brick, white-trimmed house is a fine example of Classical Revival design. Jefferson planned the 35-room home in 1770 and finished building it in 1809. He stocked it with many; ingenious gadgets. And of it, he wrote: "All my wishes end where I hope my days will end, at Monticello."

most important invention of all, Jefferson thought, and, inasmuch as it preserved the vast correspondence through which he speaks to us, it was.

In 1960, after touring Monticello and testing each gadget, President Harry Truman stood on the broad lawn. Looking up at the lovely dome of the mansion on the mountain, Truman murmured, "I don't see how he could do and be so many things."

Neither do other Americans. But along with genius, Jefferson was born with a robust constitution, which he respected and exercised. He did things immediately when he thought of them; he had innate good taste, faith in his fellow Americans, abounding joy in the universe, and an optimistic outlook. Late in his life he wrote John Adams: "My temperament is sanguine. I steer my bark with Hope in the head, leaving Fear astern. My hopes, indeed, sometimes fail; but not oftener than the forebodings of the gloomy."

(There are three stages in which to approach Jefferson, as if, indeed, traveling the Virginia terrain: first through his own words, *Jefferson Himself,* a volume quarried by Bernard Mayo from Jefferson's 100 volumes; then, Merrill D. Peterson's one-volume biography, *Thomas Jefferson and the New Nation,* and, finally, Dumas Malone's multi-volume life, a Blue Ridge range.)

To read Jefferson is to have the exciting pleasure of watching a great mind at play, touching issues of our own day. He appreciated, for instance, the women's role. Writing in 1771 about the plan of reading he had formed for his daughter Martha, he observed that he was "obliged to extend my views beyond herself and consider her as the head of a little family of her own. The chance that in marriage she will draw a blockhead I calculate at about fourteen to one, and of course that the education of her family will probably rest on her own ideas and directions without assistance. With the poets and prose writers I shall therefore combine to a certain extent of reading in the grave sciences. . . ."

You need know only one thing about Jefferson, an admirer once noted, and that was his insatiable curiosity, and only one thing he said, when, describing the University of Virginia's mission: "This institution will be based on the illimitable freedom of the human mind. For here we are not afraid to follow truth where ever it may lead, nor to tolerate any error so long as reason is left free to combat it."

Two strains contend. One harkens to the status quo, for things as they are, or as we would like to think they were. The other, which received a powerful shove from Jefferson, is for things as they ought to be. Over much of the course, the contest may seem one-sided, with mediocrity prevailing. But the Jeffersonian quickening is like the first word in *Genesis* that set the works in motion, the light that played over the deep. It will never subside. Jefferson and his peers struck boldly for the ideal, which, after all, is the most practicable in being not for the moment but all time.

Two miles from Monticello is Ash Lawn, designed for James Monroe by Jefferson. A chimney divides within the house to serve fireplaces in two separate rooms, and, so doing, forms an arch over the entrance-way through which Monticello can be seen across the valley.

At 18, after two years in the College of William and Mary, Monroe became an officer in the line in the Continental Army. At 20 he was among the first to cross the Delaware and, leading a charge in Trenton, was wounded in the shoulder. How could such a person be considered cautious, even tedious?

Yet nobody quotes James Monroe, not even a line from the oft-mentioned Monroe Doctrine. Summaries of his life generally characterize him as the first career office-holder. And he did have a sense of precinct.

But in Liberia, Monrovia the capital testifies to his concern with the problem of slavery and efforts to solve it through colonization. And Jefferson sent him to Paris in 1803 to close negotiations for the Louisiana Purchase, and, moreover, called him friend. Monroe and James Madison, said Jefferson, were his "twin pillars of happiness."

No one has any reservations about Madison's capacity. In 1790 Jefferson called him "the greatest man in the world." Living at Montpelier in Orange County, he was Jefferson's closest friend, collaborator, and, for some of the senior partner's wide-ranging projects, balance wheel.

Madison's mind illumined what he studied from the time he was a member of Virginia's last Revolutionary Convention in 1776. A newcomer, he would not speak from the floor; but, Edmund Randolph observed, he was "enviable in being the few young men who . . . could content themselves with throwing out in social discourse jewels which the artifice of a barren mind would have treasured up for gaudy occasions." Even then, though, when George Mason's Declaration of Rights proposed only religious toleration, Madison worked successfully to have it broadened to guarantee religious freedom.

Twelve years later when the Virginia convention to ratify the Constitution met in Richmond, Madison defended the Constitution against Mason's stubborn attacks and Patrick Henry's oratorical charges. Cool little Madison took the floor as if some thought had just come to his mind, and spoke quietly, holding his hat before him, and looking casually in the crown, which contained his notes.

Early in their partnership, Madison guided Jefferson's statute for religious freedom through the General Assembly. And near the close, Jefferson had Monroe and Madison serve with him as three of the six visitors for the new-founded University of Virginia. "This, if it succeeds, will raise up children to employ Mr. Madison's attention through life", Jefferson wrote John Adams.

No other institution ever had such a board. (One must be careful of sweeping assertions. Somebody

James Monroe
Ash Lawn look
on Monticello

Thomas Jefferson designed President Monroe's 'Cabin Castle' in 1798 and built it the next year. The home is only two miles from Monticello. The 16-foot marble statue of Monroe on the lawn was by Attilio Piccirilli. Commissioned by the Venezuelan government, the sculptor finished the statue after a revolution had brought to power some officials who did not appreciate the Monroe Doctrine. Piccirilli's work gathered dust in a New York studio 50 years. Then Jay W. Johns of Charlottesville rescued the statue and brought it to Ash Lawn. Michie Tavern below, was purchased by John Michie from John Henry, Patrick Henry's father. The Inn's oldest part was built before 1740.

JAMES MONROE.
1758–1831

Rotunda heads the 'academical village' drawn by Jefferson for University

Cavaliers and coeds play on the University of Virginia's vast green Lawn in Charlottesville. Statue of Thomas Jefferson stands before the Rotunda. Jefferson designed the campus centerpiece as a modified adaptation, to half scale, based on the Pantheon in Rome. It served as a library and numbered Edgar Allan Poe among its patrons. William Faulkner stalked the Lawn as a resident lion. Jefferson, though a seer, scarcely could have foreseen students sailing frisbie spheres around spherical Rotunda, but the plastic frisbie might have interested him at least momentarily.

in Charlottesville once remarked on the presence of three Presidents in the same company. You mean *four* Presidents, interjected a member of the local gentry. When those around him, puzzled, asked who was the fourth, he said, "I'm the President of the Albemarle Possum Club.")

Even as the Colonies were breaking away from Britain, Jefferson was working to write a Revolution in Virginia's statutes. "Our Revolution," he wrote later, "presented us an album on which we were free to write what we pleased."

The time for fixing every essential right on a legal basis, he wrote in the Revolution, "is while our rulers are honest, and ourselves united. From the conclusion of this war we shall be going downhill. It will not then be necessary to resort every moment to the people for support. They will be forgotten, therefore, and their rights disregarded. They will forget themselves but in the sole faculty of making money, and will never think of uniting to effect a due respect for their rights. The shackles, therefore, which shall not be knocked off at the conclusion of this war will remain on us long, will be made heavier and heavier, till our rights shall revive or expire in a convulsion."

Jefferson initiated a five-man committee to revise all Virginia's laws and then with George Mason did most of the work. He succeeded in abolishing the laws of entail and primogeniture through which the great planters had passed along their estates intact. Having knocked the prop from under an aristocracy of wealth, he proposed to substitute an aristocracy of talent through a system of public education.

"I think by far the most important bill in our whole code is that for diffusion of knowledge among the people," he wrote George Wythe in 1786. "No other sure foundation can be devised for the preservation of freedom and happiness. Preach, my dear sir, a crusade against against ignorance, establish and improve the law for educating the common people. Let our countrymen know . . . that the tax which will be paid for this purpose is not more than the thousandth part of what will be paid to kings, priests, and nobles who will rise up among us if we leave the people in ignorance."

In 1817 he still was striving through his friends in the General Assembly to establish public schools, "a bantling of forty years' birth and nursing," and when the General Assembly again rebuffed him, he turned to the idea of creating a state institution of higher learning, "the last act of usefulness I can render . . ." With thousands of Virginians migrating to the western frontier and to eastern cities, Jefferson saw the University as a means of restoring Virginia's creativity.

He struggled five years to coax appropriations through the General Assembly, designed the academical village around the lawn with the Rotunda as the centerpiece, devised a curriculum of electives, supervised the hiring of a faculty, shaped the board of visitors, and presided over the construction of the buildings.

Monticello's overseer, Edmund Bacon, left a description of Jefferson, then in his 80s, sticking the first peg in the ground for the construction.

"After the foundation was completed," Bacon wrote, "they had a great time laying the cornerstone. The old field was covered with carriages and people . . . Mr. Monroe laid the cornerstone. He was President at that time. He held the instruments and pronounced it square. He only made a few remarks . . . and several others made a speech. Mr. Jefferson — poor old man — I can see his white hair just as he stood there and looked on.

"After this he rode there from Monticello every day while the University was building, unless the weather was very stormy. I don't think he ever missed a day unless the weather was very bad. Company never made any difference. When he could not go on account of the weather, he would send me, if there was anything he wanted to know. He looked after all the materials, and would not allow any poor materials to go into the building if he could help it. He took as much pains in seeing that everything was right as if it had been his own house."

How did his bantlings fare?

Jefferson's dream of a system of public education did not become a reality until 1870, the product of the first General Assembly during Reconstruction. (Had it come earlier, in Jefferson's day, it might have assured an educated electorate that would have had the sense to stay out of the Civil War.)

The University, which he envisioned as a capstone for public education, became, without a foundation of public schools, an essentially private institution. In this century it began to improve and Colgate Darden Jr., after he left the Governorship to become the University's president, bolstered the curriculum, added some 15 buildings, and stimulated Virginia high school students to come to Charlottesville. President Edgar F. Shannon Jr. continued the revival so that the University began to assume the role Jefferson envisioned.

"As I grow older," said Darden, "I am surer than ever that the people are the only reliable guardian of their affairs, and that our great responsibility is to educate them for this important task, since each generation must demonstrate anew its capacity to govern."

Darden then shifted his attention to the public school system, and, as a member of the State Board of Education, working with Lewis Powell Jr. and others, preached the necessity of strengthening the poorer localities' offerings for their children. The 1973 General Assembly adopted state standards, with funds to help achieve them. For a moment, anyway, Virginia was back on Jefferson's track. There would be, of course, relapses, as well as gains, but that would give others something to work on, and, as Jefferson said, "The earth is for the living."

The Valley of Virginia

Virginians speak casually of the Valley of Virginia. Sometimes they do not bother to define even in their minds the ground they cover. Usually they are thinking of the Shenandoah Valley, which extends roughly from a point north of Winchester on the Maryland-Virginia line southward to Buchanan County.

But the Valley, the *Great* Valley, extends across the State to Bristol and beyond. Within the State, the Great Valley is divided into four main sections: the Shenandoah Valley; the Fincastle Valley from Buchanan to Christiansburg; the Dublin Valley from Christiansburg to Marion; and the Abingdon Valley to the Tennessee line. Along the way are numerous local valleys, so that when a Virginian says he is from the Valley, he opens a vista.

The huge trough lies between the Blue Ridge, the backbone down the center of the State, and the Alleghenies to the west of Staunton. The Blue Ridge is the older range, as ancient, indeed, as any in the United States. Even to the mountains Virginians have to be first. Once a vast sea lapped at the Blue Ridge's western slopes. And when the hills barely hump their backs above the white morning mists, it seems that the waters have come again.

Squiggling along the top of the Blue Ridge, as if poured from a cake-decorating cone, is the 105-mile Skyline Drive, running through Shenandoah National Park, which claims 60 peaks that rise 3,000 to 4,000 feet. From Hogback Overlook a visitor can count 11 bends in the Shenandoah River. At Afton, Skyline Drive changes its name to the Blue Ridge Parkway and continues under that alias 217 miles to the North Carolina border.

In the fall Virginians flock to the Skyline Drive and marvel at the Blue Ridge's rainment in shades of red, orange, yellow, bronze, and purple. The effect, as with camouflage, is to render a most substantial mountain into a wavery, vari-hued veil that could be parted with the hand.

Sweeping across the Valley floor in a broad swath is Interstate 81, never far from old U.S. Route 11 that visits towns along the way. The debate over whether to take the high, low, or side road is by no means easily settled.

From 81 the motorist can watch the Valley's walls widen to 20 miles at some stages and narrow dramatically at others until at Buchanan, where Purgatory Mountain thrusts from the northwest, the Valley constricts to 1.5 miles.

Interstate highways are supposed to save time, but the traveler can become so bemused with the double panorama that he is apt to miss his exit and travel 20 or more miles too far.

Old 11 and new 81 crisscross the Indian Warriors' Path which became the route of the Great Philadelphia Wagon Road down which tramped thousands of immigrants from England, North Ireland, Scotland, and Germany.

At Roanoke (then called Big Lick) the Wagon Road split. The Carolina Road made its way through Fancy Gap into North Carolina, and the Wilderness Road continued through Southwest Virginia and into Kentucky.

The immigrants tended to light together, like flocks of birds, which accounts for the Germany flavor of such Valley towns as Strasburg and Woodstock and the Scotch-Irish character of Staunton and Abingdon. The tough-sinewed newcomers came to be known as Cohees — from the Quakers' "quote he" — while the inhabitants east of the Blue Ridge were Tuckahoes, named for an Indian root.

From 81, 11, or the mountain drives, the motorist can drop into a variety of scenery, including the Apple Blossom Festival in Winchester.

A product of the Roaring 20s, the Festival includes the crowning of Queen Shenandoah, the daughter of a celebrity, atop Handley High School's steps, a pageant, and a grand parade that unwinds four hours under the batons of such disparate

*In Berryville is
Rosemont, where U.S. Sen-
ator Harry F. Byrd
lived from 1933 until
his death in 1966. He en-
couraged tourists to
enter the estate and stroll
amid flowering pink
and white dogwood and
flaming azaleas.
The custom persists. The
mansion has an eight-
columned veranda across
the front, where
Byrd's Senate colleagues
gathered every spring
to enjoy the Virginian's
hospitality, concluding, invariably, with old-
time strawberry shortcake.*

Visitors walk in Rosemont, Byrd's old home

Winchester's
Apple Blossom
Festival of-
fers pageantry

When the apple trees bloom in the orchards around the town of Winchester in early May, more than 100,000 persons gather to revel in three days of events unfolding at the Shenandoah Apple Blossom Festival. The extravaganza offers a pair of stunning parades. A fireman's parade, featuring new and old pieces of firefighting equipment from throughout the United States, unwinds its gleaming coil during an evening. Next day the Grand Parade begins in the afternoon. Dozens of bands across the country contend for a place in the 50-year-old spectacle's five-mile-long line of march. Some 300 contingents attend from the Nation's high-schools and colleges. The floats are bedecked in thousands of flowers. Spectators pack rows of bleachers along the procession's route through Winchester.

Queen Shenandoah and Court watch children re-enact pageant

Winchester Apple Blossom Festival culminates in the crowning of Queen Shenandoah on the steps of John Handley High-School. National celebrities take part in the parades as marshals. Such disparate personalities as evangelist Billy Graham and sports commentator Howard Cosell have appeared. Presidents of the United States have watched.

Among Winchester's other attractions is a building of hewn logs, covered with clapboard that George Washington used as his headquarters while surveying Lord Fairfax's land.

On a Sunday, May 15, 1864, while Lee and Grant were heavily engaged in Spotsylvania County, Union General Franz Sigel set out from Winchester with the idea of destroying the railroad at Staunton; but Confederate General John Breckinridge rushed to meet him at New Market with several brigades, bolsteved by 257 cadets from the Virginia Military Institute in Lexington. In a charge through an orchard and across a pasture, the youths captured a Federal battery. Ten cadets were killed and 47 wounded. Now a Hall of Valor sits on the heights and displays many mementoes celebrating the bravery of the Blue and the Gray. Periodically, Civil War buffs fervent congregate to re-enact the Battle of New Market. There is much firing, bursting of smoke bombs, charging around by the actors, and cheering by the audience that lines the hillside, but nobody dies.

Youths stage
mock battle
at New Market
where VMI
cadets fought
in Civil War

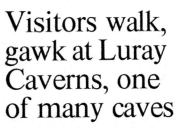

Visitors walk, gawk at Luray Caverns, one of many caves

Virginia mountains abound in limestone caverns. Some, equally entrancing, are Endless featuring a Hindu Temple; Grand a Santa Claus; Skyline posing Rainbow Falls, Dixie a Castle on the Rhine. Shenandoah has a Capitol Dome, and Massanutten a long, long hall; Cudjo offers a walk under two states, and Melrose soldiers' names on walls. On the next page, in Staunton, is the Manse, where President Wilson was born.

personalities as evangelist Billy Graham and sports commentator Howard Cosell.

Most such rites are motivated by politics in Virginia, but, paradoxically, the Apple Blossom Festival in the heart of Byrd country always has been nonpolitical. Indeed, though the Festival originated in a regional chamber of commerce, neither does it have a commercial air. There is an unworldly innocence about the whole event. Probably the explanation is that people love a parade, and the Apple Blossom Festival's is tops.

In nearby Berryville is Rosemont that was the home of U.S. Senator Harry F. Byrd. During the Senator's lifetime, drawn by a sign that said VISITORS WELCOME, tourists walked the winding paths amid flowering white and pink dogwood and flaming azalea, often puzzling whether they had happened upon a public park or private preserve. Sometimes, knocking at the door of the broad veranda, they met the chunky Senator, ruddy-faced and blue-eyed, who would escort the strangers around the grounds, identifying trees, shrubs, and flowers and pointing to the distant Blue Ridge where he loved to hike.

Another sign on the drive said LOOK OUT FOR DOG, not warning of a watchdog but cautioning the visitors to drive carefully for the dog's sake. A black cocker spaniel, Candy, tagged after the Senator everywhere, to the tops of mountains and into his office at the Capitol and once to his seat in the U.S. Senate Chamber. Vice President Nixon, presiding that day, said, Harry, I love you, and I know you love that dog, but perhaps we shouldn't grant him the privileges of the floor.

On weekends, when he breakfasted in his pajamas, and visitors came to the door, old Byrd escorted them over the estate, unconcerned, in his pajamas. Travelers from Maine or the mid-West took home the fond recollection of the wide-chested Senator from Virginia padding pajama-clad over the grass, through the trees, pink and white petals falling about his laughing face.

In his cordiality to whoever came his way, as with so many of his habits – his love and acquisition of land for orchards, his bouts with Presidents, his insistence on economy, his curiosity about nature, his naturalness about being himself – he resembled William Byrd II; and U.S. Senator Harry Byrd Jr. closely resembles his father.

Through the Valley, using streams as augers to bore and shape the limestone, Nature has tried its hand at architecture. Its best known work is Natural Bridge that impresses, surprisingly, by its airiness, "so elevated, so light, and so springing as it were, up to heaven," wrote Jefferson.

The initials G. W. – attributed to George Washington – are carved 23 feet up one wall, and, if, indeed, Washington did it, then he set, as in everything else, a high standard in grafitti. A sign says the initials may be seen "directly in front of you," but

Seven limestone columns, Natural Chimneys, towering 120 feet, were named by settlers for stacks on old blast furnaces. Legend says two feisty gallants once fought here for a fair lady's hand. Today's horsemen, more sensibly, don't unhorse one another but charge pell-mell along the track and attempt to spear small rings suspended from the crossarms over the long course. The annual jousting tournament, "America's oldest continuous sporting event," takes place every August. The tradition originated in 1821.

Mount Solon's Chimneys draw knights to tournament

some persons stare and stare, and say, "Where? I don't see it! Where?", and others, bored, say, sure, they see it, without looking.

The Bridge is the thing. Nothing man can do, short of blowing it up, can demean it.

A scholar from the east, doing research, asked a local farmer if he had seen the bridge.

"Seen it!" he said. "I built it!"

At Mount Solon in Augusta County are the Natural Chimneys, seven limestone columns carved long ago by the Shenandoah's swirling waters. Rising 120 feet above a green meadow, they resemble a turreted castle, a resemblance enhanced during the annual jousting tournament in August. Men on horses ride pell mell along a course and try to spear free-swinging rings suspended from horizontal cross bars.

What a treat it would be to see Launcelot come charging, armor-clad, onto the field, looking for Guinevere.

The Valley is honeycombed with caves tunneling around in the earth's innards, each bend of a corridor offering a strange metaphorical landscape. It is impossible to pick the weirdest underground landscape. Each cave has special features.

Two of Skyline's most prominent mountains are the Peaks of Otter. Others in Virginia are higher – Mount Rogers in Southwest Virginia soars above 5,000 feet – but the pair are set apart from the chain, a couple that doesn't wish to go along with crowd, and further, offer a contrast in themselves, Flat Top a level summit, and Sharp Top a peak tumbled with boulders so as to seem a natural rostrum for apostrophizing the universe.

At New Market one comes upon another battlefield. VMI cadets were rushed into the Confederacy's thinning ranks and captured a Union battery and helped turn back the Yankees under General Sigel. Later, Federal General David Hunter bombarded the school. After the war, VMI won an indemnity of $100,000 from the United States – and spent it building a chapel, the most martial sanctuary ever conceived, which it dedicated to Stonewall Jackson and filled at the front with a gigantic painting of Cadets charging across New Market's pasture.

A Hall of Valor, an interesting structure on the order of an overturned washtub, embraces the entire Civil War and all Yankee tourists that come down the pike. Many never heard of the War. That is the South's revenge, now that it has laid the burden aside, to make the North feel rotten about having won.

No spot is more beautiful than the others in Virginia, but if you ask the question, most persons would find room among their nominations for Goshen Pass, a five-mile gap cut through the mountains by the Maury River filled with gray boulders and blue, rushing water.

The river glides by green meadows, plunges

Natural Bridge in Rockbridge County, spans 215-foot gorge cut by creek

Lordly Natural Bridge, a 90-foot arch of limestone, was once the property of Thomas Jefferson, who bought it for 20 shillings, constructed a cabi for guests, and provided an album for them to sign. Tradition holds that George Washington as a youth clambered 23 feet up the wall to chisel his initials for posterity. Perhaps he performed in the same spirit in which he chopped down his father's cherry tree, allegedly. The bridge bears a broad highway on its back.

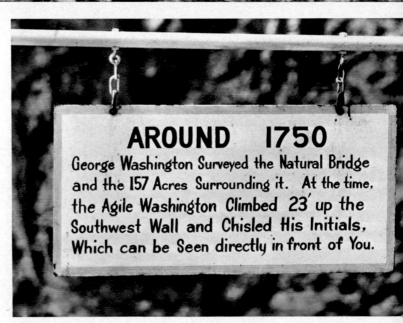

AROUND 1750
George Washington Surveyed the Natural Bridge and the 157 Acres Surrounding it. At the time, the Agile Washington Climbed 23' up the Southwest Wall and Chiseled His Initials, Which can be Seen directly in front of You.

Washington and Lee, VMI dwell side by side peacefully

George Washington gave Liberty Hall Academy 200 shares of James River Canal Company stock and a good reason to change the name to Washington Academy. After the Civil War, Robert E. Lee became its president, and after his death, his name was coupled with Washington's in the school's name.
In Lee Memorial Chapel, at right, is E. V. Valentine's marble recumbent statue of General Lee. Next door are the crenellated battlements of the Virginia Military Institute.
A statue honors Stonewall Jackson, who taught physics at the VMI before he found fame and death on the battlefield.

through rocky runs, and drops out of sound into canyons made by the mountainsides. In the spring rhododendron and laurel, or mountain-ivy, blossom along the walls.

Returning from exile in Mexico, Matthew Fontaine Maury taught at Virginia Military Institute. He loved Goshen Pass, and, dying, asked his wife, "when you take me through Goshen Pass, you must pluck the rhododendron and the mountain-ivy and lay them upon me."

They did, and later placed a monument, with anchor and chain, in the Pass honoring: "the pathfinder of the seas... who first snatched from ocean and atmosphere the secret of their laws."

On adjoining campuses in Lexington are the ionic columns of Washington and Lee University and the mustard-colored battlements of the Virginia Military Institute, looking as if Athens and Sparta dwell side by side, an interesting symbiosis. As Cadets pass the W&L campus, they salute the Chapel where Robert E. Lee lies buried. W&L men used to late-date the Cadets' girls on weekends after the soldiers had gone to quarters. The indignant VMI men called their neighbors "minks" after a beast of reputedly loose behavior; the W&L men dubbed their rivals Keydets. Each accepted the nickname conferred by the other. The Cadets liked Keydets, and the W&L men did not object to being likened, they said, to a highly valued species draped about the fair sex's neck.

In 1798 George Washington endowed the school. In 1865 Lee accepted the trustees' bold offer to become president of the tottering college. (The trustees had to borrow the suit in which their emissary extended the bid to Lee – and then, after Lee agreed, borrow $1,500 for the General's salary.) One of Lee's disarming traits was his refusal to accept others' worshipful evaluations of himself. In taking the assignment at Lexington rather than other far more lucrative offers, Lee said, "I have a self-imposed task which I must accomplish. I have led the young men of the South in battle; I have seen many of them die on the field; I shall devote my remaining energies to training young men to do their duty in life."

Stories about his presidency are as numerous, enduring, and upright as the University's massive white columns. Reproving a student for poor grades, Lee remarked, "We do not want you to fail."

"But, General," said the boy, "you failed."

"I hope you may be more fortunate than I," said Lee quietly.

He proved an innovative educator, and after his death the trustees coupled his name with Washington's in the University's.

In Lexington is the Robert E. Lee Episcopal Church. When strangers express surprise and say they thought an Episcopal church always was named for a saint, Lexingtonians murmur, "Oh, but it is!"

In Goshen Pass the blue-green Maury River flows past rocks

A youth dives from a boulder into a deep pool formed by the Maury River in the Goshen Pass. Others sun on the rocks under green mountain wall. The river is named for Matthew Fontaine Maury who became so fond of it while teaching at the Virginia Military Institute that on his deathbed he requested that his body be taken through the gap o the way to Richmond.

Blue Ridge Parkway offers horses, hills, cider for sale

The Peaks of Otter are by no means the highest mountains in Virginia, but they are among the most popular. Their fame springs from the fact that they stand apart from the others in the Blue Ridge a pair of showoffs. Flat Top is 4,001 feet high,

and Sharp Top is 3,875. By comparison, Virginia's highest peak, Mount Rogers in the far Southwest, is 5,719 feet high. Sharp Top has a spectacular crest of rocks, and vacationers climb there to watch the sun rise, over the mountains, a beautiful, impressive view. John Randolph of Roanoke was so moved by the moment that he commanded his servant to join him in prayer. There are other rewarding sights around the Peaks including rhododendron and an occasional elk.

On the campus next door are stories about Stonewall Jackson, "Old Tom Fool" while he was a physics professor at VMI before the war. Once Major Jackson was drilling cadets when a storm broke over their heads and they broke for shelter without his command. In the barracks the youths crowded at windows to see what the Major would do. He stood at rigid attention, amid the downpour, sword drawn, until the drill-period ended.

VMI's battle cry originated before the battle of Chancellorsville when Stonewall, seeing so many former pupils around him, observed, "The Institute will be heard from today!" A fight song about the school's never-say-die attitude concludes: "That's the spirit of VMI!" Superintendent John A. Lejeune, who did not attend the Institute but was familiar with *esprit de corps* as a Marine General, once remarked to VMI alumnus J. Addison Hagan that "VMI is the greatest fraternity I ever knew."

A prominent member was George C. Marshall, born in Pennsylvania. Once, weary of hearing old classmates boast about being native Virginians, Marshall muttered that, well, anyway none of them had an arch named for him at VMI — one of the few times he ever showed a trace of vanity. Now a research library there also bears his name.

Typical of Marshall was the way he retired as Chief of Staff. He telephoned the Secretary of War and got instead Assistant Secretary Kenneth Royall. The Secretary was away, reported Royall.

Marshall was sorry, because, he said, he was going to retire at the end of the day and had wished to say goodbye to the Secretary.

A flustered Royall telephoned President Truman. "Did you know George Marshall was going to retire," asked Royall.

He most certainly hadn't, said the President.

Well, he is, said Royall, he's cleared away all the odds and ends, and he's leaving in an hour or two.

What was Royall going to do for a ceremony?, demanded the President.

It was too late to do anything properly, said Royall.

"You'd better by a damn sight do something about it!" said Truman.

(Royall related the story to former Governor Colgate Darden when the two were on an advisory group to the National Security Council.)

So Royall had secretaries call every department in the Pentagon and instruct the entire force, from janitor to General, to assemble in a mall. President Truman came over and expressed the Nation's indebtedness to the retiring Chief of Staff, and Marshall thanked him. And then the General put on his hat and went home to Leesburg.

That was the spirit of George Marshall.

Lexington was the home of U.S. Senator A. Willis Robertson, known for his contributions to the Nation's fiscal system. Closer to his heart were his efforts at conservation. They sprang from a boyhood reading the *Leatherstocking Tales* and a life-time hunting and fishing around Virginia.

"As a boy I hunted a great deal with the town blacksmith," he once remembered. "One day I couldn't go with him, and later I asked, 'Blacksmith, what luck did you have?'

"'Oh' he said, 'I didn't do too well. I shot 10 times and killed 10 birds and a darned old rabbit'."

"One Saturday a hunter killed 85 quail on the Blackwater River. In those days the farmers would trap 'em, and I've seen bunches hanging in the butcher stores like bananas, two for a quarter."

"When I entered the State Senate in 1916, I knew we weren't going to have anything left to hunt unless we had some laws." He helped organize and then headed Virginia's game and fish commission and sponsored conservation laws in Congress.

At Staunton is the Manse, where Woodrow Wilson lived until he was eight months old. Then his father accepted a call to a Presbyterian church in Georgia. North Carolina and Georgia claimed Wilson but during the 1912 Presidential campaign, he declared: "I am a born Virginian."

His reading and writing United States history may have inspired his wish to align himself solidly with the Revolutionary War Virginians. Not since Madison presented the model for a Constitution had anyone come forward with statecraft to match Wilson's plan for a League of Nations.

At any rate, if Wilson didn't stay at the Manse much beyond infancy, the foundation has collected enough memorabilia to make it seem that he never left. And to understand Wilson and the close, affectionate, reverent family from which he came, it is helpful to visit the Manse and hear the chimes in his father's church a block away.

Wilson himself returned in December, 1912, for a birthday party. His remarks at the townspeople's banquet demonstrate his feel for metaphor and a politician's knack to weave, while gazing into well-fed faces, a theme:

"Men believe now that sooner or later their wrongs are going to be righted, and that a time is going to dawn when justice will be the average and usual thing in the administration of human affairs.

"You may imagine the pleasure, therefore, that it gives me to come back to the place where these standards cannot be questioned, for these standards were first established, so far as this side of the water is concerned, in Virginia. And no Virginian can stand up and look the history of Virginia in the face and doubt what the future is going to be. If I have any advantage as a Virginian, it is merely that I have got a running start. A man that ties in with communities of this sort began further back and the further back you got your start, the greater the momentum. And all that is needed is momentum. It does not need any cunning tongue. It does not need eloquence. It just needs the kind of serenity which enables you to steer by the stars and not the ground."

Star and stag

When the traveler leaves a plane at the Roanoke airport and looks at the mountains rimming the tableland he feels a moment as if he has stepped in the center of a circus act. They easily are the most antic mountains in Virginia. They appear to be turning cartwheels, walking on stilts, somersaulting, and doing joyous handstands all around the horizon. To complete the illusion there is to the west a long, flat-topped mountain, sloping sharply at both ends, and sagging a mite in the middle – a circus tent. This is Tinker Mountain, near Hollins College, and was, long ago, the haunt of a hermit tinker, who dwelled in a cave and mended pots and pans. Every year in the autumn, on unannounced Tinker Day, Hollins dismisses classes, and students climb the mountain back of the school and perform skits, an occasion in keeping with the capering mountains around Roanoke and an improvement in scenery over the bushy-visaged tinker.

The circus motif continues. When the traveler approaches downtown Roanoke, he spies a mountain in the shape of an elephant slumbering smack in the center of the city, its trunk curled before it, wandered away from the circus. Further, on its forehead is mounted a huge white star, the kind of trapping elephants wear when they amble through dust around the track of Ringling Brothers and Barnum and Baileys Circus. This is Mill Mountain.

The traveler who comes unexpectedly upon the star at night is not likely to forget it. On a plane, glancing out the porthole, he is taken aback at what apparently is a comet at his elbow. Or approaching on Interstate 81, which sweeps through the city, the motorist suddenly sees looming through the mists above him a beacon on a building that must outtop anything in New York or Chicago.

The star was unveiled – or turned on – Thanksgiving Eve, 1949. The speaker, former Representative Clifton A. Woodrum, for whom the airport is named, likened it to a star of peace. The star first arose in the minds of the Retail Merchants Association as a different kind of Christmas ornament, but once illuminated, it continued to shine. Roanoke became the Star City. The star weighs 10,000 pounds, contains more than 2,000 feet of neon tubing, is 88 feet in diameter, and is supported on a structure tall as an 8-story building. Some Roanoke residents would like to take it down. But it is a natural expression of exuberance by a city that was once a frontier town named Big Lick.

Sharing the mountain crest are several features, including a children's zoo and the Mill Mountain Playhouse. City planners have ambitious designs on the summit; meanwhile, one has the satisfaction of glancing up at any time in Roanoke and seeing the elephant that is a mountain.

On Jefferson Street, moreover, before the EIKs Club is a noble bronze stag, with round light bulbs socketed in the tips of its antlers. Urban renewal may dispose of the stag; meanwhile, it is an object of delight to children who pass by – or to anyone who has enough of the child in him to find pleasure in the droll or unexpected. During some Christmas seasons the white bulbs have been replaced with lights of red, green, blue, orange, and yellow, and the stag has borne a glowing Christmas tree on its head.

Maybe urban renewal will find a place for the stag. The City showed good sense in retaining, and refurbishing, a municipal market that had been in existence since 1885. When planners in other cities wonder what to do to revitalize downtown, they might look at Roanoke's market, heaped with vegetables, fruit, and meat from the Valley and bustling with shoppers.

The Roanoke River swings through the town, and the visitor comes upon it in surprising places, much as if it is a brook, instead of a stream wide as a four-lane highway, brimming to the banks, lined here and there with huge trees, and running easy as you please through the town. Finally, the Norfolk and Western Railway tracks bisect the town, which means that trains are ding-dinging through the center of things all day. What with mountain, star, stag, river, market, and trains, everything seems first-hand in Roanoke, immediately felt.

The railroads built Roanoke.

As recently as 1880 Roanoke was not Roanoke but only the small town of Big Lick, named for a marsh of salt deposits that lay just east of the present Norfolk and Western Railroad Shops.

In 1881 word spread that two railroads, the Shenandoah Valley and the Norfolk and Western, were looking for a junction.

As Council considered inducements to bring the railroads to Big Lick, John C. Moomaw set off on horse to Lexington to confer next day with the railroad officials. A rider met Moomaw at Buchanan next morning with the message that Council offered a terminal and $10,000. Moomaw galloped to Lexington with the bid and the railroads came to Big Lick. In 1882 the town dropped the name Big Lick in favor of Roanoke (Indian for wampum), befitting its jump in population from 700 in 1881 to more than 5,000 in 1883.

Later, the discovery of rich seams of coal in Southwest Virginia assured the Norfolk and Western's success. Its coal-loading piers at Lamberts Point in Norfolk are the world's largest, and the rail line ties the two cities and their fortunes together.

Roanoke has suffered depressions as well as booms. Maybe it is some of the old Big Lick in its background that helps it bounce back.

In 1958 the American Viscose Corporation Plant, one of the largest artificial silk factories in the world, shut down and threw more than 5,000 out of work. Roanoke's unemployment rate rose to 11 per cent. But local businessmen reformed the Viscose property into the Roanoke Industrial Park and went searching for prospects. Now the Roanoke area has more than 200 industries.

In 1966 the Roanoke voters approved a bond issue for a new civic center and then in 1967 authorized $22.6 million for municipal improvements.

The gleaming white civic center – the coliseum seating more than 11,000, plus a vast exhibit hall, and the auditorium, seating nearly 2,500, and shaped on its top deck in the flowing curve of a grand piano – generates excitement in its promise and may be taken as expressing Roanoke's elan.

The city relies heavily upon leaders recruited from graduates of Roanoke College, which is in adjoining Salem. (Established in 1842 near Staunton, it moved two years later to Salem.)

Further, Roanoke, from the time it was a stop on the Great Wagon Road, has been a young man's town. There is no such thing as a newcomer in Roanoke. A week, a day, and he is an old-timer. Finally Roanoke is the gateway to Southwest Virginia's Mountain Empire.

Eight-story star on Mill Mountain shines over Roanoke

Norfolk and Western Railway freight cars line tracks entering downtown Roanoke, headquarters for the prosperous railroad. Stag raises antlers, adorned with light bulbs, before EIKs Club on Jefferson Street. Star, built in 1949, has 2,000 feet of neon tubing.

In Radford each summer is an outdoor drama, *The Long Way Home* by Earl Hobson Smith, a true account, which gives an insight into the stamina of Southwest Virginia. It portrays a pioneer, Mary Draper Ingles, the first white bride west of the Alleghenies.

On a midsummer morning in 1755 the Shawnees struck Draper's Meadows, near what is now Blacksburg. They tomahawked Mary Ingle's mother, shot and killed two men, wounded Mary's sister-in-law, Betty Draper, and snatched and killed her baby. Mary fought like a wildcat and saved her two sons.

The Indians marched the captives through the wilderness to Ohio, where Mary made herbs and sewed shirts and proved too useful to be killed. Then the Indians separated her from her boys, George and Thomas, and sent her to work at Big

Bone Lick making salt in brine vats. Hearing that the Shawnees planned new attacks on Virginia settlers, she resolved to get back, somehow, and warn them. She and a Dutchwoman made a break in late October, carrying only a blanket, tomahawk, and knife. They lived for weeks off berries, roots, and nuts. The Dutchwoman, driven by hunger, tried to strangle Mary, but she fought free, found a log canoe, and escaped.

On the forty-third day she staggered into a corn patch near Angel Cliff in Giles County and called weakly for help. A friend heard and recognized her, carried her in the house, and reunited her with her husband, who had been searching for her and the boys. Their son George died soon after he was taken from his mother; Thomas was ransomed after 13 years. Betty Draper was ransomed after six years.

107

The Dutchwoman survived and was returned to her family in Pennsylvania.

Mary and William built a new home at Ingles Ferry, where she bore him four children and lived until 83. That was the stock that settled Southwest Virginia.

There was little difficulty restoring the clay-chinked, one-room log cabin — with dirt floor, potato hole, and fireplace; without windows — in which Booker T. Washington was born a slave on a Franklin County plantation near Hale's Ford.

Soon after the Emancipation Proclamation, when he was nine, his mother moved the family to Malden, West Virginia. The child learned the alphabet from a Webster's Blue-back Spelling Book, and at 12 entered school, working each day five hours before class began and then returning to the mines or salt furnace after school. When his teacher asked him his name, he knew only his first, but, noticing that the other children had two, Booker calmly said "Washington," believing, he wrote later, that ought to make him "equal to the situation."

Hearing two miners discuss a school for blacks in Virginia, he determined to go to Hampton Institute. He walked 500 miles, working his way at odd jobs, sleeping under the planks of the sidewalk in Richmond. Told at the school to sweep a classroom, he swept it three times and dusted it four. "I guess you will do to enter this institute," said the teacher. That thoroughness characterized his life. He combined a fierce drive with well-nigh saintly forbearance for others.

In the late 1950s, blacks found him a controversial figure, an Uncle Tom, some said, for not advocating forcefully civil rights. However, his famous speech in Atlanta at the International Exposition of 1893 was aimed at whites as well as blacks. He depicted a ship, lost at sea for many days, suddenly sighting a friendly vessel and signaling: "Water, water; we die of thirst." The answer from the friendly vessel came back, "Cast down your bucket where you are." A second, third, and fourth signal for water was answered the same way. The distressed vessel's captain, at last heeding the injunction, cast down his bucket, and it came up full of fresh, sparkling water from the mouth of the Amazon River.

Washington's advice for blacks was to do their utmost with what jobs they could find in their communities and for whites to cast down the bucket of opportunity and education among the eight million blacks "whose habits you know, whose fidelity and love you have tested in days when to have proved treacherous meant the ruin of your firesides."

The metaphor has application today through John Gardner's concept, preached through Common Cause, of excellence in every occupation. Indeed, seeing that our lives hinge on his skills, with what rejoicing do we discover, for instance, an automobile mechanic who knows what he is doing.

At any rate, the rapidly increasing number of blacks in Virginia government, helping enact and administer laws through elected and appointed offices in county, city, and State, is growing assurance that the blacks will cast down their buckets on a parity with whites.

Among persons consulted by the Virginia Commission on Constitutional Revision in 1969 was S. W. Tucker, Richmond civil rights lawyer. A commission member asked Tucker what he thought of amendments they were proposing for the Virginia Bill of Rights. That document didn't need much changing, replied Tucker. "All you have to do," he said, "is add three words: We mean it."

Virginia has nearly 100 lakes of varying dimensions but most are man-made.

The largest lake within Virginia's borders is Smith Mountain Lake. (Buggs Island Lake, which is larger, slops over into North Carolina.)

Smith Mountain Lake covers 20,000 acres in a square formed by Roanoke, Rocky Mount, Danville, and Lynchburg. Most of it lies in Bedford and Franklin Counties. On its 500-mile shoreline, the 40-mile-long lake offers such diverse features as a yacht club, a State park, and a wildlife refuge.

Writing to a friend in Lynchburg, Thomas Jefferson said of the city: "I consider it is the most interesting spot in the state, and the most entitled to a general patronage for its industry, enterprise, and correct course."

Numerous industries from manufacturers of overalls to atomic reactors have taken Jefferson's attitude. But even before he pointed out its advantages, indeed, before there was a single dwelling, 17-year-old John Lynch saw the place as a likely site for a ferry, and established one in 1757. John, a Quaker, took no part in the Revolution, but his brother Charles, a Colonel in the militia, did enough for both. He maintained law and order by stringing Tories by their hands to a tree limb and lashing their bare backs until they yelled "Liberty Forever!" — a summary justice that gave rise to the term "Lynch Law."

The more peaceable John added a tobacco warehouse on the bluff above the ferry, and thereby laid the town's economic foundation. Farmers rolled in hogsheads of tobacco, lowered them on ropes from the warehouse to bateaux, which floated them down the James River to Richmond.

About 1810 farmers began bringing tobacco in loose leafs to Lynchburg's warehouses for auction, a system that spread to other sales centers. By 1827 a dozen manufacturers were at work in Lynchburg, among them the picturesque Colonel Augustus Leftwich, an Englishman who came to the city at 18 and made his fortune. He strolled through his factory like a potentate, dressed in white linen, with a slave behind him holding aloft a green umbrella.

Thanks to the leaf, on the eve of the Civil War Lynchburg was rated on a per capita basis second

Virginia Tech students frolic on drill field

One-room cabin stands on the spot where Booker T. Washington was born into slavery on a Franklin County plantation near Hale's Ford. Visitors may see methods of farming that were used during Booker's childhood. In an Atlanta speech, he urged blacks and whites "to cast down your buckets where you are." At least that philosophy worked well enough for Booker T. Washington.

to New Bedford, Mass. as the wealthiest town in the United States.

The period after the war brought John W. Carroll, who won the basis of his fortune and the name of his most famous brand in a card game. An orphaned youth, newly arrived in the city, he staked his last cent on a single jack, which won the pot. In gratitude Carroll called his number one chewing tobacco "Lone Jack."

In 1882 James A. Bonsack, who lived between Lynchburg and Roanoke, manufactured a cigarette making machine that revolutionized the industry. It produced 120,000 a day, equivalent to the output of 40 expert hand rollers. A Lynchburg firm manufactured Bonsack's machine until he sold the patent to the Dukes of North Carolina. Thereafter Lynchburg's role as a tobacco center diminished, but other industries — shoes, foundries, pulp and paper mills, textile and garment factories, medical supply firms, milling — took up the slack.

Lynchburg was shaped by the James River. Its main streets — Court, Church, Main, Commerce — run parallel to the James on four giant terraces cut by the river on its course through time. So Lynchburg residents walk and ride where the river ran, a fact said Lynchburg historian Philip Lightfoot Scruggs, that gave him a good deal of satisfaction as a child. The river was Lynchburg's city planner.

The city's landmark is Monument Terrace, a granite and limestone grand stairway, a continuation of Ninth Street, which ascends the steep 70-foot hill between Church and Court Streets. Along the way are 13 landings, where the climber may pause and pant. Crowning the summit is the Courthouse.

In John Lynch's day a meandering path led from the ferry up "the Hill." Later it was strewn with cinders, and then, after the completion of the Courthouse in 1852, paved with cobblestone steps.

In 1883 the town placed a 20-foot cast iron fountain at the foot of steps to honor four firemen and a policeman who had lost their lives in a fire. The sun shone on the fountain that sprayed over the red shirt and Alice Blue pants of a cast iron fireman. The Daughters of the Confederacy placed the figure of a Rebel infantryman at the top of the hill so that the way was well and colorfully guarded. In 1922 the city moved the cast iron fireman to Miller Park, and replaced that statue at the foot of the hill, with a bronze one, "The Doughboy" by Charles Keck, honoring Lynchburg youths who had served in World War I. It also voted to replace the cobblestone steps with granite and limestone and change the name from Courthouse Hill to Monument Terrace.

The terrace, an imposing edifice, laps down the hill like a dollop of syrup over stacks of pancakes. Lynchburg residents, climbing it, pause to rest, and sun themselves, and look at the city at their feet. It still is a center for ceremonies. When presidential candidate Dwight D. Eisenhower came whistle-

stopping through Virginia in 1952, his train stopped at the foot of Ninth Street hill, and he, his party, and newsmen came out of the cars and looked up at the hill which seemed to be heaped with faces, packed pale, pink, and close together as a pile of beans. Politicians began issuing communiqués about carrying Virginia.

They need never have doubted Lynchburg, which has the reputation of being one of the Commonwealth's most conservative cities. Former City Manager Robert D. Morrison recalls that in announcing the area's first successful fund drive for Lynchburg College, he turned to the Bible to characterize his city: "Prove all things. Hold all things. Hold fast to that which is good."

The public drive for the college was long overdue, he told the audience and added: "On some occasions Lynchburg requires a little too much proof."

Still, the City Manager himself was evidence that Lynchburg has been blessed in this century with an able and progressive administration.

And Lynchburg College, along with Randolph-Macon Woman's College and Sweet Briar, provides a leavening of youthful ideas and attitudes.

Lynchburg College began as Virginia Christian College in a remodeled hotel in 1903 and changed its name and charter in 1919. Randolph-Macon Woman's College opened on a campus overlooking the James in 1893 and set its course by becoming the South's first independent college for women to start a chapter of Phi Beta Kappa. Sweet Briar which opened in 1906, was guided by Dr. Meta Glass for 41 years. Her zest for learning and sense of humor did not dim in that long span.

Miss Glass wore her many honorary wreaths as lightly as a spring hat. Newswoman Eudora Lyell recalled how a student in a nearby male college once addressed a note blindly to Box 406 at Sweet Briar: "I'm wondering," he wrote, "what the holder of my box number at Sweet Briar looks like. As for me, I am tall, dark, and I drive a Ford V-8 ... I am a freshman ...
What class are you in?"

Miss Glass penned a reply: "I am tall, too, and not as thin as I once was. My hair is white, and I drive a Buick. I was a freshman in 1896. You ask what 408 at Sweet Briar looks like. From the recent picture of me in the public press at the time we

Lynchburg rises along terraces carved by the James River

Elevator, far left, behind City Hall, whisks travelers to Courthouse at top of the Ninth Street hill. Skyscraper in background is Allied Arts Building. Opposite City Hall is Post Office. Looming behind Post Office is New Fidelity National Bank. The spire on Monument Terrace is First Unitarian Church. Doughboy holds post at bottom on Church Street, Confederate soldier guards way before Courthouse crowning hill.

established the Carter Glass chair of government, I think I look like nothing human."

Dr. Glass concluded by inviting the freshman to visit her if he happened to be up that way. (The witty college president was the sister of the peppery U.S. Senator Carter Glass, who led in the founding of the Nation's Federal Reserve System.)

Among other outstanding Lynchburg natives was Dr. Douglas S. Freeman, biographer of Lee and Washington. Rebecca Yancey Williams caught the lighter side of the South in *The Vanishing Virginian*.

Dr. R. Walter Johnson, a physician, pioneered during his spare time in developing black athletes and successfully overcoming color barriers in tennis. He converted part of his Lynchburg home into a training camp for youngsters and helped shape, among a score of champion tennis players, Richmond's Arthur Ashe.

The city has gained enormously from the activities of the Lynchburg Christian Fellowship, an ecumenical service organization sponsored by more than a dozen churches, and led by two ministers, P. G. Cosby III and Beverly Cosby, sons of a leading businessman.

In 1966, 16 churches of eight denominations joined in buying a rambling old house on Madison Street as a center – Kum-Ba-Yah (Come by) – for community programs: a coffee house for teenagers, tutoring, scouting, arts and crafts instruction, classes in home-making and typing for adults, programs for invalids and retired persons, and counseling for unemployed, school dropouts, alcoholics, and broken families. It also sponsors a summer daycamp for children and has financed construction of apartments in the central city. The Fellowship is reaching into every problem in the city. Through their vigorous support, Lynchburg churches demonstrate they intend to hold what is good.

Near Lynchburg is Poplar Forest, the retreat designed by Thomas Jefferson to escape the horde of guests that descended on Monticello, not only domestic, but foreign as well since anyone who came to America seemed impelled to look him up.

In Jefferson's eight-sided home, four rooms, also octagonal, open off a hall 20-feet square, lit by a skylight. While superintending construction, Jefferson was thrown from a horse, and, during his recovery, found time to write his *Notes on Virginia*.

It used to be that Virginians would speak of *the* University with the understanding that the only State-supported University was Mr. Jefferson's in Charlottesville. So when T. Marshall Hahn, President of Virginia Polytechnic Institute, began speaking of VPI as the University, Eastern Virginians thought it an affectation. They were accustomed to thinking of VPI as a curious combination of cow college and military school and were startled to discover in the 1970s how it had multiplied into more than 100 buildings.

On the heights they found a series of high-rise dormitories, a giant limestone screen, well-nigh a maze, folding this way and that, soaring nine stories, shorn at the roof line of Gothic ornament but still derivative of the Tudor decor of the older campus in the plain below. Set on the plateau, stark and white, they convey a sense of the Alamo – Alamo Gothic.

The Blacksburg school began with the "War of the Colleges," the contest among 24 Virginia schools to obtain land-grant aid as soon as the State was restored to the Union. The winner was a late starter, Preston and Olin Institute, a small Methodist school founded in 1851 in Montgomery County. On October 1, 1872, it opened the doors of one building as the Virginia Agricultural and Mining College with four teachers and 43 students. Legend says that a Craig County youth strolled into the building merely to look around and came out, bewildered enrolled, with a State scholarship in hand.

The school caught the fury of postwar politics with the Readjusters firing the faculty, including the President, when in 1880 they won control of State government; in 1886 the Democrats regained control and dismissed everybody on the faculty again. Then the scene settled and VPI began its long pull. The greatest impetus for it, and other State schools came during the 1966 General Assembly that se about to overcome long-standing deficits in education.

But the heart of the VPI campus has not changed. It is a 22-acre drill field, a shallow green bowl surrounded by Gothic halls, the most imposing one being Burruss Hall, named for a long-time president a craggy precipice of a building, praised and denounced, but either way, striking, facing south an overlooking the center of the drill field.

Whit all the buildings shouldering the sky, VPI most refreshing architectural feature is that vast peaceful, tree-fringed field.

At class break the bowl becomes alive, as if a the energies of the university were pouring into i boys and girls in all kinds of dress, hair style, an attitude crisscrossing the field, animating its spa cious face, dramatizing with their youthful presenc the purpose of the great gray buildings.

At one time or another during each day, nearl every one of the 13,200 students crosses the fielc The scene is endlessly diverting. A Breughel woul go wild at that moving, mile-square canvas of figure: No wonder that architects laying out the master pla in 1922 decreed the drill field "an expanse to b left open forever."

The past is in the bowl – presidents and professor who gave their energies, alumni who remembere alma mater, politicians who wrote yellow-backe bills that were translated into the gray-white stone on the hills. But mostly, viewing the hurryin; laughing, talking throng, one sees on the field future in which educated men and women will shap the world into a better, fairer place for all person

Mountain Empire

Ask a visitor from another country or state what portion of the Commonwealth he likes best and the odds are heavy that after a moment's reflection he will say Southwest Virginia.

Because of the mountains?

No, he says, the people.

Here is a paradox: Virginia's most over-exploited and under-developed region is the one that most often wins outsiders' admiration.

Are the people so different there, that they inspire in visitors a tenderness that borders at times on being a protective feeling?

Apparently so.

Of course, we are dealing in generalities. Southwest Virginia has its share of mean-minded individuals.

But it also seems to have more than its share of sweet-spirited persons.

Still, feeling this, the visitor distrusts his own instincts; and so, chancing to meet someone else who has traveled Virginia, he asks offhandedly what the stranger liked best about the State, and the man answers, a little defiantly as if he doesn't expect to be believed: The people of Southwest Virginia. The two rejoice and fall to swapping observations.

Directness is the word that best sums them up, forthrightness in feeling, speech, and deed. There's little or no impediment between what a Southwest Virginian feels and what he says and still less between what he says and does.

To solicitous outsiders, many Southwest Virginians seem to lack armor. Yet many in the Mountain Empire mix shrewdness with their disarming warmth. Joseph Smiddy, President of Clinch Valley College in Wise, is Virginia's only college president to charm a swimming pool out of the Governor's touring budget committeemen by telling stories and serenading them with a dulcimer. (The droning dulcimer, a three-string instrument, has a burr that betrays its Scottish origin.)

Ted Dalton of Radford, the Republican who rolled up impressive returns in two campaigns with little or no party east of Roanoke, simply sought to embrace all the voters he could reach. The tall, drawling Dalton would put his long arm around a State official heavily committed to the Democratic Organization and pull the hack to him in a bear hug, and hold him until onlookers seemed to see the hostility spilling out of the squirming Democrat.

Bob Porterfield, when the Depression hit Broadway, brought a troupe of 22 starving fellow actors to his home town of Abingdon and created Barter Theatre where play-goers swapped vittles for tickets. The most precious commodity that Porterfield bartered was a generous, exuberant spirit.

He had what he called his "in-the-hole committee" members on whom he could call in an emergency, such Samaritans as Lady Astor, Jesse Ball DuPont, and Paul Mellon.

Not until 1946, 14 years after Barter's curtain had gone up, did the General Assembly appropriate $10,000 as its first contribution to the Nation's first state-subsidized Theater. In the early years 90 per cent of the box office receipts in Abingdon was produce, sometimes of an exotic quality. Two mountaineers once brought in a rattlesnake.

"If they have the energy to catch it, we'll take it," said Porterfield.

Among Barter alumni are Ernest Borgnine, who drove a truck in the first of his five years with Porterfield and began by playing Rosencrantz in *Hamlet;* Patricia Neal, from a nearby Kentucky mining town who moved directly from Barter to Broadway, and Gregory Peck, who played John Brown in the first act of *Lee of Virginia* and reappeared after the hanging as Stonewall Jackson in the second act.

Porterfield housed the actors in the abandoned Stonewall Jackson Institute for girls. A rugged man with leonine features, he supervised the troupe's members as if they were students in the erstwhile

Deep pink rhododendron run riot across Haw Orchard Mountain bolder strewn pastures in the sky. Haw Orchard

114

t Rogers State Park in far Southwest Virginia. The highland park encompasses the Commonwealth's highest crests.

Crowd packs Old Fiddlers' Convention

Old-timey and blue grass bands play in Felts Park at Galax. As many as 30,000 congregate for four days of festivities in Southwest Virginia. Fiddle, banjo, bass fiddle, mandolin, guitar, and home-made dulcimer have their place on the stage. Players warm up in the rea of the tent, and then*

come forward into the spot-
light to take their
turn at playing for prizes.
The cash is small,
but then the honor is large.

*Musicians play on
at Old Fiddlers' Convention
as spectators lounge
under the sun at Felts Park,
storing up memories in
mind and on film and tape
recorder. Old-timey
musicians stress the tune;
blue grass group
often features the vocalist.
Old-timey favors
the fiddle, and blue grass
leans on the banjo.
Anyway, musicians play on.*

118

Felts Park Meadow is packed with tents, trailers, cars, and campers. And the musicians play on. Before and after they make their pitch on stage, they gather in groups about the park to sound an A and pick a tune. They bend intently over the instruments as if they are extracting the essence of life from the strings.

Each band attracts its own audience. Late at night the clog dancer takes the stage. His upper torso remains motionless while his legs engage in a furious shuffle as if on marionette strings. When the clogging is done, the crowd scatters to tent and motel. Sometimes square dancers start in the parking lots, and musicians play on 'til dawn.

Galax is known worldwide for mountain music and greenery

119

Virginia's high country has wind-pruned trees and Mabry's Mill

Mabry's Mill on Blue Ridge Parkway is a favorite stop for hungry tourists. The mill old grinds grain as it did when Ed Mabry ran it years ago. Mabry and his wife Lizzie worked three years in West Virginia for money to build the mill. Mabry also had blacksmith shop, sawmill, and wheelwright shed in industrial complex. Emulating handy Mabry, the Park Service has rebuilt an old whiskey still, sorghum press, an apple butter apparatus, mint still, and soap-making kettle to show how mountaineers lived. In the autumn visitors may purchase apple butter and syrup, but moonshine is not for sale. Scene at left is in Mount Rogers State Park. Mount Rogers looms in the background like a blue whale on the horizon. It rises to a grand height of 5,719 feet, and is the State's highest peak.

seminary and he was the old-maid dean. "Do whatever you please where you live," he told newcomers, and then added: "But I don't like sin!"

So that Barter Theatre would go on, Andrew Miller, Virginia's Attorney General, persuaded Porterfield to form the Barter Foundation, instead of relying completely on the in-the-hole committee and its founder's infectious personality.

Each evening before the curtain rose, "Mr. P.", as his actors called him, gave a brief performance down front to warm up the audience. In 40 years it never varied. He presented the person who had come the longest distance a pair of locally manufactured Mary Gray Nylon Hose. Then he thanked the audience and concluded: "If you like us, talk about us, and if you don't, just keep your mouth shut!"

His voice always rose and cracked a little on the word "just" and broke up the house.

Porterfield's idea was natural for a native of Southwest Virginia where barter was frequent. Even yet the visitor sees trading posts in small towns. Further, Southwest Virginians are accustomed to having to go away to survive – and to returning as soon as possible. They long ago proved that you can come home again. Many exiles live for the time they get back to the mountains.

Periodic mining depressions disperse families throughout the Midwest and even to the West Coast. A Southwest Virginian finds a job in Detroit City, Dayton, Kansas City, Cleveland, Evansville, or Gary, and sends for his family and friends. Gradually members of an entire church congregation have moved to another state and then sent for the preacher to join them. They try to carry Virginia with them.

In Wise, they tell of a man who had worked all his life in a sawmill, cutting one stand of timber and moving to clean out another until finally none were left, and he went to Dayton to hunt for work in "the ice box factory," the refrigerator plant.

"You fellows from Southwest Virginia are fine workers," said the plant's personnel manager, "but the trouble is you don't stay long. Just as soon as we finish training you, we look up and you're gone back to Virginia. Would you promise to stay?"

"Yessir," said the old sawmill hand, "I sho' will stay with you. I'll stay til you clean this place, and then I'll hop you move!"

In some industrial centers the concentration of Southwest Virginians is larger than that of the population in the town they left behind – and to which they vow to return. The boarded-up church in the hollow is waiting.

With special feeling the exiles from Virginia sing a favorite hymn:

This world is not my home, I'm just a passing thru,
My treasures are laid up somewhere beyond
the blue;
The angels beckon me from heaven's open door,
And I can't feel at home in this world anymore.
I have a loving mother up in glory land,

Alleghenies' broad rampart overlooks the Great Valley

A mountaineer went away one day to the big city to work in a factory making refrigerators, boxes, or something, and the pay was not bad, better than at home, anyway, but in a little time he went to the manager and said he was leaving the icebox factory, going back to the hills, and the manager asked why. The mountain man said, well, the pay is better here, but the day is better there.

Blue mountains offer white bouquet of rhododendron

On the Blue Ridge Parkway near Buena Vista an azure, tilting sea of mountains bears a spray of rhododendron. The landscape out there is never still. It seems in constant motion, up and down, a kaleidoscope of angles to catch and delight the eye, an eternal jumble reaching back to the horizon and blending with the sky. In summer the lush foliage carpeting the ridges is so thick as to seem impenetrable. The leaves rustling in the breeze make a mountain seem a living thing. The passing motorist feels that he could

reach out and touch
the mountain's rough flank.
One day, he prom-
ises himself, he will stop the
car, get out, stroll,
and investigate the cool,
shady, other world
that lives beneath the trem-
bling green canopy.
And so he hurries on his
way, and never does.

State Street divides the city of Bristol

In Abingdon, at right, is Barter Theatre, founded by Bob Porterfield during the Depression. He brought hungry actors from Broadway and admitted patrons to plays for anything they cared to bring in the way of food. It was a nourishing exchange for mind and body. Barter Theatre still flourishes, the play goes on, but most customers pay cash. Below, State Street partitions Bristol between Virginia and Tennessee.

The Washington County Courthouse's white columns grace Abingdon's Main Street. A tiffany window in blues and greens, a World War I memorial, adorns the Courthouse. Abingdon began as a fort on the frontier.

I don't expect to stop until I shake her hand;
She's waiting for me now in heaven's open door,
And I can't feel at home in this world anymore.

The glory land of which the Southwest Virginians sing is not the hereafter but the home they left behind — and to which they revert at every opportunity: when they're laid off, or have a vacation, or, burning the roads, on their weekends and holidays.

"And always, without exception," Delegate Edgar Bacon of Jonesville once said, "they are brought back when they die."

In the far Southwest, the Virginia triangle's sharpest point thrusts into Tennessee, Kentucky, and West Virginia. Cumberland Gap and other cuts in the mountains were the jumping off places for Virginians heading west. They continue to take those routes out. Eight counties will lose at least 10 per cent of their population by 1980 and even more by 2020, State planners predict.

The Commonwealth is losing one of its greatest natural resources. A West Virginia University sociologist, Dr. John D. Photiadis, found in a study in 1972 that after Appalachia's mountain residents move out, they also tend to move up, "through plain hard work and the use of conventional avenues that our society provides."

Still, Southwest Virginians who have lived in other states or other sections of the Commonwealth for 10 years or longer often feel that they are on detached service from their true homes.

The invisible but unbreakable tie explains, in part, anyway, the abuse of the absentee or mail ballot in the Mountain Empire. The mountaineer marking time in Fairfax or Norfolk is more interested in what is going on in the precinct he left behind him. He welcomes the candidate, or the candidate's aide, who comes to get his ballot.

Working the mail ballot has become known as "black satcheling," for the black bag which the bag man carries. Clinch Valley College President Smiddy has recorded the phenomenon in a ballad:

Yonder comes that black satcheling man,
He's got all the mail votes he can stand;
He's back from Nobleville where he voted Uncle Bill,
He's a politician from the old Southwest!

The rest of the State's politicians had a difficult time fathoming abuse of the mail ballot among a people whose ethics on other matters were unusually high. At times an exasperated General Assembly would threaten to abolish absentee voting.

It fell to legislators from the Southwest to try to interpret their neighbors' feelings to their irate colleagues in the State Senate. The Southwest Virginias abroad had been forced from the hills they loved by an economy which was not of their own making or understanding.

"Their heart is in these mountains," said one, "they vote here and they come home, as I say, when they can."

127

Boys study Abrams Falls cascating down limestone terraces. The mighty waterfall, cleared by a modest creek, is in S

128

Virginia, eight miles west of Bristol. In woods nearby is Little Abrams Falls, which is often mistaken for big brother.

That the Appalachian people put any hope in the political system is remarkable. Only recently has it shown much concern with them.

In a vivid, sensitive portrayal, *Yesterday's People,* the Rev. Jack Weller describes how the booming outside world thrust itself on Appalachia in the 19th century's last quarter.

Representatives of wood industries invaded the mountains to buy virgin timber that covered the ridges and slopes. Unused to bargaining in a money economy, the mountaineer often sold trees up to eight feet in diameter for a dollar apiece. Next, purchasers of coal deposits invaded Appalachia, and the mountaineer sold his property for as little as 50 cents an acre.

The deprivation continues. Clinch Valley College President Smiddy tells of saddening visits to Appalachian graveyards: "When you count in those little mountain cemeteries the graves of the boys killed in Vietnam, it really makes your heart heavy. You can see who pays. The mountain youths are not advised in the ways of escaping the draft. Only a small percentage go to college, and, of course, many volunteered because of a lack of opportunity in their communities or from patriotism. But then if you join the army and you haven't been trained, you get a rifle and go to the front. That's happened in every war we've ever had. They've always gone, from the Battle of King's Mountain to today."

Yet the visitor to Southwest Virginia is aware not so much of the residents' hardships as their humor. The stories, as well as their lives, often center on the church.

They tell of Rawhide Baptist Church which had come into some unexpected funds. The deacons held a meeting to decide what to do with the money. "I'll tell you what let's do. Let's buy a chandelier," said one brother.

Whereupon another arose and said, "I object. In the first place it's a strange word, and nobody can spell it, and in the second place, even if we got a chandelier, nobody would know how to play it, and in the third place, if we're going spend a lot of money, what we really need around here is better lighting!"

In another church in the hills a visiting preacher droned past noon until an old fellow on the front row drew out a pistol and placed it in his lap. The preacher promptly brought the sermon short. Later, as the congregation was filing out, the preacher asked the pistol-packer, "You wouldn't have shot me, would you?"

"No," said the old man, "but the fellow who invited you here is in deep trouble."

Often the stories are accompanied by music. Strings sing through the mountains – the fiddle, guitar, banjo (or banger), the bass fiddle, mandolin, and lastly, but first, really, because it came over with their Scotch forbears, the dulcimer.

Many log houses still abide in far Southwest Virginia hills and deep valleys

Music festivals abound through Southwest Virginia. College youths flock to them, drawn by the region's relaxed acceptance of life as well as by the music. Mountain people look curiously at Ivy League youths who wear long hair, beards, beads, and bluejeans, but they pass no judgment. The big cities' concrete caverns can produce no individuals rarer than some originals living in Southwest Virginia's hollows.

Granddaddy of the festivals – oldest, largest, loudest, longest – is the Old Fiddlers' Convention in Galax. It tuned up in 1935 when 872 people gathered in the high school auditorium. The Convention grew and moved to the meadow in Felts Park and now the town's population of 7,500 quadruples during four days in mid-August as pickers and fiddlers begin arriving on Thursday and play until sunrise Sunday.

Players and applauders fill the bleachers, pack around the bandstand before a twin-peaked tent, and overflow into a vast parking lot. Rising behind it all is the majestic silver vat of the town's Carnation milk plant.

On the floodlit stage contestants vie more for the honor than the cash prizes of $2.000. But the music is not confined to the bandstand. Five-piece bands warm up all over the park and continue to play after they make their pitch. Nor does the music end there. Galax motels resound with the plinking, plunking, skirling strings. A band climbs on the back of a flatbed truck in a motel parking lot and sets to playing, and a square dance blossoms on the asphalt, a shifting, swirling, interweaving kaleidoscope of colors and patterns. It is musical fission. Once Galax was known for mountain greenery, the tiny heart-shaped galax leaf, which carpets the crests surrounding the town, and is exported to florists around the world. Now it has become synonymous for evergreen music.

130

If a plantation symbolizes
Tidewater aristocracy,
then the log house stands
for the pioneers
in Southwest Virginia who
built their first
home with one basic tool:
the axe. One man
could finish the job in a
short time. At left, on
Groundhog Mountain, is
the home of Aunt Orelena
Puckett, mountain midwife,
who lived to be 102,
and ushered 1,000 babies
into the world. When
the heights were icy, 'Aunt
Arlene' pounded nails
through her shoe soles and
made her way to the
expectant mother. She last
attended the birth of
her grand-grand nephew in
1939, the year she
died. The cabin was built
in 1870. Below, workers
in Mount Rogers State Park
construction ice house.
An old abandoned log cabin
clings to the hillside.

Natural Tunnel winds its way through stone mountain

At left, cavern swallows a railroad, some telegraph lines, and Stock Creek. Tunnel's mouth is 100 feet high and the wall. inside range up to 175 feet apart. Tunnel curves 850 feet through rock. At right, the tunnel opens into huge rock-walled chasm more than 400 feet deep, 600 feet in diameter, and 3,000 fee around the rim. Natural Tunnel and chasn are in Scott County, 14 miles from Gate City.

In the knots of players and spectators spread through Felts Park one comes upon the giants of mountain music, who have their recordings cached in the Library of Congress and the Smithsonian Institution.

The players are divided, but amicably, between those who favor old-timey music or square-dance tunes and those who prefer blue grass of the sort popularized by Earl Scruggs and Bill Monroe and his Blue Grass Boys.

The old-time musician plucks the fifth string with his thumb and brushes the rest with the backs of his fingernails, clawhammer style; the blue grass performer picks the instrument with two fingers and thumb. In old-time music the dominant instrument tends to be the fiddle; blue grass gives the banjo a major solo role. Old-timey tends to be danceable; blue grass, singable.

The vocalizing during an old-timey tune usually is a fast stream of well-nigh senseless words to the beat of the band, a commentary shouted quickly to get out of the way of the stampeding music:
I went over to old Joe Clark's,
Old Joe wasn't at home,
I ate up all the ham meat,
And left old Joe the bone.
Or
I'm gonna tell you sompen,
Sompen I don't need,
A crosscut saw, a mother-in-law,
And 44 chickens to feed.
Or
Anything happen that I don't come
And you kill that dominicker,
Save me some.

Old-timey purists wouldn't even play *Country Roads,* the West Virginia anthem. They insist that the blue grass instrumentalist uses the tune to show off his own virtuosity, and the old-time player shows off the tune.

Folk ballads are old-timey. And now the best of blue grass is producing today's folk ballads. To hear a ballad in the mouth of a mountain girl, clear, sweet, true, is like listening to a bird on a bough.

Further confusing distinctions is a third style, Western, or country music, rural pop that ranks on the disk jockey's charts. Blue grass and country both stem from old-timey, and to tell the three apart on paper is impossible. You have to listen.

In the dark meadow, the players' faces are white blurs, the curved neck of the bass fiddle rising over the group like a charmed serpent, the crowd around them intent, silent, and the hard-driving music calling to mind strong horses galloping across a plank bridge.

In the distance a voice on the public address system is blaring to all fiddle players to keep moving right on in the tent, and the crickets in the grass are chirping away at their own convention.

Finally at about 1 a.m., the clog dancers come on stage one by one.

The clog, or flat foot.

How to describe it.

Scholars say it goes back to the caper of the Old English morris dance.

Maybe.

Or it could be a body is so ecstatic his feet won't stay still.

The clogger's upper torso remains motionless while feet and legs fly about as if on marionette strings. Sometimes the dancer turns his hands slightly at the wrists, resembling, in a girl, a preening motion.

At times the dancer seems to be sliding barefoot on marbles, trying to pick them up with his toes.

Individual styles are in high contrast.

A teenager is all kinetic energy, dancing on one foot, seeming to defy gravity.

The crowd roars at his agility, but those who have been there before look down the program and say, Wait, and, when a fairly heavy-set man in his 50s comes on stage, Watch!

The middle-aged man from Mount Airy, simply dressed in a white shirt and dark trousers, his graying hair close-cropped, is a disciplined artist, his feet moving so rapidly they blur like humming-birds' wings, scarcely seeming to move, and, meanwhile, his body is still, and he is turning his head slightly, casually, this way and that, his chin tilted, so that, although his feet are in a furious shuffle in one spot, he gives the impression of man strolling at ease in a garden, looking idly at the flowers.

On a Sunday in spring summer and fall the motorist on the Blue Ridge Parkway spies a picnic every 200 feet; but if a body have no hamper, he must have a destination – one simply does not drive hundreds of miles to look at other people picnic – and his goal usually is the best-known structure on the Parkway: Mabry's Mill, and, if October, the Mill's home-made apple butter and fresh squeezed sorghum.

All his life a Virginian hears about Mabry's Mill-Mabry's Mill, and at last, badgered by his wife, he veers 150 miles off course to view it. As he pulls into the parking lot before the rustic coffee shop and gazes on a sea of automobiles, he realizes that everyone else has heard about it too.

In the rush into the shop for food the mill is nearly forgot, but, emerging, fed, one notices it, aloof, serene, by the quiet pond, fit for a jigsaw puzzle on a shaky card table.

Ed Mabry, with his saving wife Lizzie, hired out as a blacksmith for nearly three years in West Virginia to earn money to built the mill in the early 1900s. With his mechanical bent, he made a one-man industrial complex: blacksmith shop, saw-mill powered by an overshot wheel, grist mill, wheelwright shed. The old mill creaks, grumbles, and groans, as it did in Mabry's day.

Scotch-Irish, Germans tramped along Wilderness Road in search of new land and a new life. Daniel Boone cut a trail throught the Cumberla Gap and lost a son in an Indian attack. But to-day the easy riders scarcely know it is there.

A massive rock chimney, a rough-hewn pyramid, is all that is left of John Newlee's foundry near Cumberland Gap. In the 1880s, the foundry's ponderous mill wheel lifted a 500-pound hammer that shaped red-hot ingots drawn from a charcoal fire Intense heat fused the blast chimney's stones. Tri-State Park in the Gap offers a view of the countryside much as settlers viewed it: a promised land.

134

Railroad tracks cut through Cumberland Gap where pioneers made their way into the West

Emulating Mabry, the Park Service has expanded the complex to embrace a mint still, soap-making kettle, sorghum press, apple butter operation, and whiskey still. The winding trail, with one display feeding into another, soon absorbs sightseers. Ed Mabry would be intrigued at the cunning fashion with which the Park Service is processing tourists, well-spaced, evenly, smoothly, where he used to grind corn.

Bristol, Virginia-Tennessee is proof that a house divided need not fall although it may be subject occasionally to a beaut of a brawl. State Street is the boundary line that partitions Bristol between Tennessee and Virginia. From the start, even when the Indians were chipping arrowheads from nearby flint deposits, the area has been a manufacturing center. In 1856 a railroad spike joined the Norfolk and Western Railway tracks with those of the Southern Railway and also connected, thereby, the Eastern Seaboard to the Mississippi. Bristol became "the Gateway to the South."

It was the gateway for a number of enterprises, including a branch of the industrious Reynolds family. When the brothers left Patrick County, R. J. went to Winston-Salem, N. C. and A. D. came to Bristol to manufacture plug tobacco. His son, R. S. founded a cleanser plant in Bristol, but when the factory burned during World War I, a scarcity of building materials prompted him to move to Louisville, Kentucky. The Reynoldses came back in 1972 to establish an aluminium fabricating plant.

Controversy over the boundary line between the Twin Cities lasted two centuries. In 1890 the dispute reached the U. S. Supreme Court. Not until 1903 did the odd couple reach an agreement when Tennessee ceded to Virginia the northern half of State Street, the new name for Main Street.

In a survey of the two, Professor C. P. Curcio of Virginia Highland Community College notes that in the early days criminals could evade the law simply by stepping across State Street. Summoned once to quell a disturbance, police from both sides found a drunk straddling the line and taunting: "Who's going to get me?" The police tossed a coin. Virginia won, so Tennessee got him.

Several summer camps operate near Bristol, and, invariably, when the trains or buses bearing the campers arrive, the boys and girls spill out of the cars and walk down the center of State Street, straddling the line, calling: "Look, I'm walking down the street in two states at the same time!"

Virginia has a personal income tax; Tennessee does not. The difference has prompted industries and professional offices to locate on the Tennessee side. (Of 54 doctors listed in the telephone director, Dr. Curcio found two with Virginia numbers.)

The two jurisdictions joined in supporting construction of a hospital, but the babies are delivered in the building on the Tennessee side, which has a high birth rate for a city its size.

Cattle browse on mountains that rise fold on fold

*Old-timers insist
cattle must be bred short-
legged on one side,
the better to stand on hills.
Green-clad mountains
are in Tazewell County in
the far Southwest. Below,
fishermen try luck in Smith
Mountain Lake near
Roanoke. Man-made, the
lake covers 22,000 acres,
has a 55-mile shoreline,
and is 40 miles long.
A smaller lake, Leesville,
covers 3,400 acres be-
low Smith Mountain Lake.*

Logically, perhaps, the state line should be moved to constitute a single city in one state, but, inquires Professor Curcio, which side would relinquish its identity?

There was, for instance, the little old lady on the Tennessee side who objected to being redrawn into Virginia because, she said, she had always heard that the climate was better in Tennessee.

The cites share an increasing number of services and honors. A seven-foot tall marble monument on State Street commemorates the Nation's first recording of country music on August 2, 1927. The session featured Jimmie Rodgers, a Mississippian, and the Carter Family from Maces Springs in Virginia's Scott County.

A little more than eight miles west of Bristol off the highway to Gate City is a scenic attraction – Abrams Falls – that has been for years one of the most impressive and least known natural wonders in Virginia. Indeed, many visitors, after walking a quarter of a mile through the woods, find a good-sized waterfall, view it dutifully, and depart without realizing that they have seen Little Abrams Falls. The big brother lies another 2,000 feet or so through the trees. Both are named for a homesteader who owned the land on which they stand, or fall. Sometimes solemn-eyed boys follow visitors to Little Abrams just to see if they have the wit to push on a few more feet.

Abrams Falls makes a spectacular splash as it cascades 125 feet into a natural amphitheater with sheer rock sides. Yet the mighty volume of water is fed by a small stream, Abrams Falls Creek, scarcely more than a brook that is not too broad for leaping. Abrams Falls reigns, a dazzling white throne in the green wood, with Little Abrams as its footstool.

Equally as majestic and nearly as unknown as Abrams Falls is Natural Tunnel, an unnaturally large hole in the ground curving 850 feet through a stone mountain and emerging at the bottom of a rock-walled chasm that looks as if it might have drained at one time all the waters in the world.

The chasm, or amphitheater, measures 3,000 feet around the rim and 600 feet in diameter. From the top of the ridge above the tunnel to Stock Creek at the foot is 350 feet, equivalent to a 35-story building.

Rising 400 feet above Stock Creek is a pinnacle, Lover's Leap, from which a Cherokee maiden and her Shawnee chief – it always is a Cherokee maiden in the stories; did the Shawnees have no daughters? – plunged at daybreak. The Park Division's brochure advises: "Watch your step going up Lover's Leap."

Daniel Boone is said to have been the first white man to walk the tunnel – how exciting to venture into that gaping hole, not knowing how far it penetrated – and lived a few miles up the Clinch River where the town of Castlewood now stands.

The tunnel's interior walls range 100 to 175 feet apart, leaving ample room for Stock Creek and a line laid in 1890 by the South Atlantic and Ohio Railroad from Bristol to Big Stone Gap.

The tunnel looms in many silent films. The figure emerging from the vast black maw usually is a comedian, legs twinklings in front of a pursuing locomotive.

Gazing from inside the tunnel one sees far away at the entrance the patch of brilliant green foliage framed by the dark silhouette of the tunnel's walls. The spectator feels a little as if he is a figure in a giant peepshow into which a large eye may be peering.

In Bristol the Eastern Virginian is disposed to feel that he has reached Virginia's outermost bounds – until he looks at the map and sees Cumberland Gap 100 miles to the west.

Sighting a limestone escarpment towering 600 feet, the pioneers knew they were only a dozen miles from the gateway to Kentucky. But the Gap itself is more of a saddle in the rock ridge, 1,648 feet above sea level, with its southwest shoulder rising another 500 feet and the northeast shoulder looming 1,000 feet. Today's motorists often drive through the Gap without realizing it, but the pioneers were well aware of every step they took through Indian territory. In 1773 guiding settlers into Kentucky, Daniel Boone lost a son in an Indian attack at the Gap.

In the Cumberland Gap National Park is a massive rock blast-chimney, and the remains of John G. Newlee's foundry. In the 1880s its wheel lifted a 500-pound hammer that shaped red-hot ingots from a charcoal fire.

Virginia's highest State park, and a contender for most magnificent, spreads across Haw Orchard Mountain, adjacent to Mount Rogers, the State's tallest mountain, which gives the park its name. In that Southwest Virginia tableland, one mountain merges into another like massive swells in an ocean. Here and there though are heaps of boulders large as houses.

This is the high country that America's Gilded Age barons stripped of virgin forests and then set the slash afire so that the mountain crests were wreathed in flames that could be seen for miles. Boulders exploded from the heat. But nature cloaked the scarred crests in rhododendron, laurel, and wild azalea. In the spring the broad landscape blooms in lavender, pink, orange, and flame red blossoms. (A clump of rhododendron atop Haw Orchard opens this section on the Mountain Empire.)

A person on top of the Mount Rogers State Park feels that he's climbed a beanstalk into a new land. When he gazes into the lowlands, marked by faint trails out of a nursery rhyme, it's as if he is totally out of touch with that busy other world.

southside mockingbird

Virginia, a Guide to the Old Dominion, the superb WPA guidebook edited by Eudora Ramsey Richardson, suggests that poet Gertrude Stein must have been traveling through Southside Virginia when she observed: "There were no houses, no people to see, there were hills and woods and red earth out of which they were made, and there were no houses and no people to see."

Gertrude is gone, her words lingering, and there still are undulating stretches of pine and sedge.

Yet, out of that lonely country, maybe because of it, sprang the liveliest instrument, the banjo.

When music festivals convene in Southside pastures, not many players realize that the instrument they prize was invented by Old Joe Sweeney, who was born in Buckingham County.

In his teens he took the ban-jar, a four-string instrument out of Africa made from the shell of a gourd, added a fifth string, and substituted for the gourd a round, wooden frame.

He founded the American minstrel show with the help of his younger brothers, Dick and Sam, and cousin Bob. Joe, who died before the Civil War, was buried at Appomattox. Sam became Jeb Stuart's personal troubadour.

Too bad Miss Stein couldn't have popped into a Southside political rally and sampled Brunswick Stew, named for the county in which it originated. Legend says a hunter, annoyed because he had to cook while the others were out shooting, simply dumped everything he could find around the camp into a big pot and let 'er stew. Anyone who has watched the day-long preparation in a 45-gallon iron pot, the boiling of the meat — chicken, lamb, or squirrel — until it pulls from the bone, and then the addition in precise stages and amounts of potatoes, onions, butterbeans, tomatoes, and corn, understands that the making of Brunswick Stew is as precise as a poem by Gertrude Stein.

Most of all one wishes the creator of "a rose is a rose is a rose" could have heard "Thirty-five — fi — fi — six — six — seven — seven — seven — eight — eight ———t!" – the chant of the tobacco auctioneer.

Southside Virginia is tobacco country and raises bright, or flue-cured, nearly everywhere, as well as some dark-fired, a small amount of sun-cured, and even a trace of burley.

Tobacco is demanding on man and land. Farmers put in plant beds for a new crop even before they begin harvesting the previous year's, which is why it's sometimes called "the 18-month crop." In the old days, when the hard-used land began to erode, planters abandoned the fields and moved to new acreage. The worn-out land frequently became the site of an "Old Fields School."

Tobacco, wrote Thomas Jefferson, "is a culture productive of infinite wretchedness. Those employed in it are in a continual state of exertion beyond the power of nature to support. Little food of any kind is raised by them; so that the men and animals on these farms are illy fed, and the earth is rapidly impoverished."

John Taylor of Caroline observed that even an old planter "would be astonished to discover how often he had passed over the land and the tobacco through his hands in following, hilling, cutting off hills, planting, replantings, toppings, suckings, weedings, cuttings, removing out of the ground by hand, hanging, striking, stripping, stemming, and prizing. . . ."

Nevertheless Virginia farmers went right on planting tobacco. And in the last quarter of the 20th century, nearly 200 years after Jefferson denounced it, tobacco still was the State's largest cash crop, fetching record high prices, and paying the farmer $1 million annually. In fact, as the State urbanized and corporate farming increased, the tobacco farmer rapidly was becoming the only remaining small, independent operator, the individual Jefferson had prized as the salt of the earth.

Tobacco farmers have "payday" in Southside's big warehouses

A tobacco farmer's labor focuses on this moment in the huge warehouse's tawny vastness. The system that seems a hurly burly is swift and orderly, the practice of centuries. Along rows of baskets of weighed and graded tobacco leaf, buyers trail

e warehouseman and
e auctioneer. Chanting at
ach pile a singsong
f numbers, the auctioneer
akes only six to 10
econds to run through bids
or each basket. He
an dispose of a thousand
ounds in five minutes
r less. The farmer has the
final word. If dis-
satisfied with the price, he
can wait for a later
sale or try another floor.
A dozen cities
across Southside Virginia
have tobacco sales.
The largest is in Danville.
Tobacco still is the
State's biggest money crop.

He brings his crop to warehouses in Danville, South Boston, South Hill, Chase City, Clarksville Kenbridge, and Petersburg. Along rows of baskets of weighed and graded leaf, buyers for domestic and foreign factories, leaf brokers, and small dealers trail the warehouseman and the auctioneer. Chanting a singsong of numbers, the auctioneer takes six to 10 seconds to run through the bid for each basket, scarcely more time than it takes to roll dice.

Worthy of a poet's attention is Hampden-Sidney College, near Farmville, the State's second oldest college, the senior private institution of higher education. The Presbyterians opened its doors January 1, 1776, six months before the Declaration of Independence. On the first board of trustees were Patrick Henry and James Madison.

Hampden-Sidney sparked the establishment of two other institutions, both in Richmond, the Union Theological Seminary and the Medical College of Virginia. Nationally known for its unusually high proportion of outstanding alumni, it produced in a recent crop U.S. Senator William B. Spong Jr., who gave Virginia six years of progressive, reasoned representation.

Though the lake was not there when Miss Stein came by, Buggs Island Lake, or Kerr Reservoir, is a delight to the eye. The landscape, slowly rising and falling, has a certain monotony in that section, which the motorist feels, and yearns for a break, when, suddenly, opening before him is an inlet from a broad, smiling lake.

Miss Stein surely heard the mockingbird on her jaunt. Neighborhoods can't sleep certain seasons for the bird's tumbling notes through the night, pure sound, resembling Miss Stein's. And amid the voices — auctioneer's, banjo's, mockingbird's — rises the politician's, which, as often as not, also is pure sound. The Southside is the land of the gift of gab, and of all speakers, the supreme mockingbird was Patrick Henry.

He made his last of many homes at Red Hill, where he is buried. Near the reconstructed house and the original law office is an Osage orange tree, largest in the Nation. The tree was 100 years old when Henry sat under it and played the fiddle for his children. He had retired.

But Washington pleaded with him to defend the Constitution against the doctrine of nullification proposed by Jefferson and Madison as the states' recourse when the Federal government exceeded its authority, as it did in the Alien and Sedition Acts.

Restless Henry had changed positions nearly as many times on the nature of Federalism as he moved residences around Virginia.

In Richmond in 1788, he opposed Virginia's ratifying the Constitution that did not spell out guarantees for individual liberties. The document, he cried, was said to have beautiful features, "but when I come to examine those features, Sir, they appear to me horribly frightful. Among other de-

formities it has an awful squinting — it squints toward monarchy. . . .

"If you make the citizens of this country agree to become the subject of one great consolidated empire of America, your government will not have sufficient energy to keep them together. Such a government is incompatible with the genius of republicanism. There will be no checks, no real balances. . . ." A bill of rights, he harped, is "indispensably necessary."

Ailing at Red Hill, the aging Henry had turned aside offers by the now friendly Federalists to become Secretary of State, Vice President, Chief Justice; but in 1796 he had written Washington that if America in his day was threatened with anarchy, he would "exert every power of mind and body" to support the government. In 1799, Washington asked him to run for the State Senate.

He spoke only once during the campaign, but the people crowded to hear him, knowing it might be their last chance. The Alien and Sedition Acts were too deep for him, he told the throng at the Charlotte County Courthouse, and might be wrong. But he denied the right of the state to rule on the constitutionality of Federal law. Virginia was to the Union what Charlotte County was to the State. Would Charlotte County have the right to question Virginia? Depicting Washington at the head of an army exercising Federal law, he asked: "Where are our [Virginia's] resources to meet such a conflict?"

The enfeebled Henry had taken two days to travel the 20 miles to the Courthouse, but, warming to the topic, the speaker became for one last time the cause. Clasping his hands, he swayed right and left, moving the audience with him as he cried: "Let us trust God and our better judgment to set us right hereafter. . . . Let us not split into factions which must destroy that union upon which our existence hangs. Let us preserve our strength for the French, the English, and the Germans, or whoever else shall dare invade our territory, and not exhaust it in civil commotions and intestine wars!"

After the speech as Henry rested in his room in a tavern, a friend reported to him the retort of a rising orator, John Randolph of Roanoke, who was running for Congress, but on the opposite side of the issue from Henry. "He is a young man of promise; cherish him," said Henry.

Contending with one another, and within themselves, the founding fathers shaped the checks and balances to uphold the central authority and yet invest the states with powers necessary to govern so vast a country and so diverse a people. If even the founders disagreed, it is no wonder the delicate balance calls for continuing adjustment in our times as well.

If Patrick Henry was among the most revered patriots, John Randolph was the most feared, at least by his foes. (The people of his district returned

Tourists view McLean House in Appomattox

A costumed hostess greets visitors to the brick farmhouse where Robert Lee surrendered his Army of Northern Virgini to Ulysses S. Grant. Below is Red Hill, near Brookneal, where Patrick Henry made his la of many homes. He played the fiddle under th giant Osage orange tree.

Visitors enter Appomattox Courthouse, which replaced original structure that burned in 1892. On a more cheerful note, Appomattox was the home of Old Joe Sweeney, who invented the banjo and founded the minstrel show.

him to Congress as long as he pleased to go.) His invective was as sudden and destructive as a shaft of lightening and marked a man forever in men's minds. There was his appraisal of Edward Livingstone: "He is a man of splendid abilities, but utterly corrupt. He shines and stinks like rotten mackeral by moonlight." And the description of his cousin Edmund Randolph: "the chameleon on the aspen, always trembling, always changing."

Randolph never trembled, nor did he change in his basic beliefs.

"I am an aristocrat," he said. "I love liberty, I hate equality."

The lightening bolts could come out of the blue at any hypocrisy. A high-born matron was expressing her sympathy for the Greeks struggling with the Turks. Randolph, pointing to black children near her veranda, said, "Madame, the Greeks are at your door!"

He freed his slaves in his will, died crying "Remorse! Remorse!", and was buried with his face to the West so that he might keep an eye on Henry Clay.

Of course, there's matter for poetry for a Gertrude Stein or any poet in the surrender at Appomattox, tragic, yet affirmative in that the long, mistaken war was done, and the Nation again was one.

On the way to Appomattox, after the Confederates suffered a loss at Sayler's Creek, General Lee told young John Wise that a few more Sayler's Creeks "and it will be over — ended — just as I have expected it would from the first." But, so expecting, he had tried four years to turn history's flank. And very nearly did.

The grave, bearded, courteous Lee was one of history's most daring gamblers, and with men's lives. The military maxim of divide and conquer became in his mind divide to conquer. He readily split his forces to outmaneuver and strike an enemy twice his size, taking long odds to reduce the odds through surprise. "How can I get at these people?" he murmured to Stonewall Jackson, as the two sat on a log in the Wilderness in the face of Fighting Joe Hooker's army massed, confident, at Chancellorsville. That time Lee divided his Army of Northern Virginia into three. He detached 10,000 under General Early to watch 47,000 under General John Sedgwick at Fredericksburg, and then, from the 42,000 Confederates at Chancellorsville, he sent 28,000 with Jackson through the woods across the front of Hooker's army to take it in the rear. For 10 hours the imperturbable Lee sat with 14,000 men under the nose of Hooker's 70,000 until Jackson struck. But in the victory the South lost Jackson, wounded mistakenly, fatally, by Southern pickets as he reconnoitered in the dusk.

In nearly every triumph Lee suffered a setback, slight or major, that flawed his plan, and, tantalizingly, just prevented his annihilating the enemy.

The North, through limitless resources, cou[ld] bumble from one defeat to another and win the wa[r].

In the Wilderness and again on the retreat [to] Appomattox, his soldiers had to restrain Lee fro[m] leading charges. The Texans in the Wilderne[ss] who cried, "Lee to the rear!" recognized that th[e] South's main chance of victory, all, really, th[at] was left of the cause, was Lee. When the Gener[al] nearing Appomattox, was pondering whether th[e] country was ready for surrender, Wise, alm[ost] shouting, told his commander that there w[as] nothing left of the Confederacy, that he, Lee, w[as] the country.

A Confederate soldier, glimpsing Lee with h[is] staff during the retreat, said that "when he di[s]appeared, it seemed as if a great light had gone out[.]"

Near Appomattox, a cluster of houses a[nd] buildings on rolling farmlands, the Confederat[es] faced Federal forces from all quarters. "There [is] nothing left for me to do but to go and see Gene[ral] Grant, and I would rather die a thousand deaths[,]" said Lee.

They met in the two-story brick farmhou[se] belonging to Wilmer McLean, in whose fields [at] Prince William County the first major batt[le,] Manassas, had started. McLean left there to esca[pe] the war, and now it was ending in his parlor.

A generous Grant ordered rations for the Co[n]federates and, at Lee's request, instructed his par[ole] officers "to let all the men who claim to own [a] horse or mule to take the animals home with the[m] to work their little farms."

Another ordeal awaited Lee as he rode back [to] his men, who filled the road, and crowded forwa[rd] to touch the iron-gray horse and rider, and cri[ed,] "Are we surrendered?" He told them, over a[nd] over, he had done his best for them, and now th[ey] must go home, plant their crops, obey the law, "a[nd] if you make as good citizens as you have soldie[rs] you will do well, and I shall always be pro[ud] of you."

And so it ended.

If, before it began, Lee had accepted Gene[ral] Winfield Scott's offer to head the Union armi[es,] then with Lee streaking up the Peninsula, [the] conflict would have ended quickly.

Or, if during the Battle of Seven Pines, a bu[llet] had not wounded Joseph E. Johnston and open[ed] the Confederate command to Lee, the war wo[uld] have lasted only a year or two. Such was the d[if]ference Lee made.

Long after it was over — the four years a[nd] 650,000 casualties — a mother presented her ba[by] son to General Lee for his blessing and asked [his] advice. Dr. Douglas Freeman chose Lee's reply [as] the words with which to end his four-volu[me] biography of the General.

Lee, who had elected to go with his belov[ed] Virginia instead of the Nation, said, "Teach h[im] to deny himself."

The new frontier

To try to comprehend Northern Virginia, you first must grapple with the population.

For three decades — 1940 through 1970 — 45 per cent of all Virginia's population increase occured in Northern Virginia.

That percentage also applies to growth in income and employment.

The population climbed from scarcely 200,000 in 1940 to a million in 1972.

Northern Virginia itself is a relatively new concept. The area extends as far south as Prince William County and as far west as Loudoun. To statisticians, it consists of the Washington metropolitan area, embracing Arlington and Fairfax Counties and Alexandria, Falls Church, and Fairfax City. Many Northern Virginians also include Prince William and Loudoun, and most Virginians are willing to concede everything north of Fredericksburg.

For years it simply was part of Virginia, with no separate designation.

That changed with the advent of Franklin D. Roosevelt's New Deal and the Federal Government's expanding role.

A second stimulus was the Nation's changing military posture with the approach of World War II. Both those developments attracted headquarters of industries that wished to be close to the making of decisions involving government contracts. The area around the Nation's Capitol received a double dose of tonic.

Slowly Virginians became aware that something was happening to the dignified, rolling countryside that began outside Washington. It was *really* rolling in a southward moving tide of subdivisions, high-rise apartments, and industries.

Sprouting like beanstalks in Arlington County's densely packed 25 square miles are vest-pocket cities. Rosslyn, an array of three dozen gleaming towers, provides a deck at the third-floor level on which pedestrians stroll from one building to another, above it all, never descending into the ground traffic. (Thomas Jefferson employed the same device in the roof-top gallery between professors' homes on the Lawn in the University of Virginia.)

In Crystal City are some 20 buildings, with those at the core connected by underground corridors. An inhabitant, if he wished, might live out his whole life without ever venturing outside.

In Fairfax County a church found it had a 90 per cent turnover in members annually. It began issuing white name cards for newcomers and yellow ones for veterans of more than six months.

The impact was felt first in the General Assembly, which began receiving requests for all kinds of special treatment for the Northern Virginians.

"What's the matter with you people up there?" the legislators asked their Washington-area colleagues.

The Northern Virginia delegation was forever trying to convey the area's growing pains to the General Assembly in Richmond and attempting to explain to their constituents why the General Assembly seemed indifferent to today. It simply hadn't dawned down State.

Northern Virginia was the first community to elect women to the General Assembly.

And while other areas were pondering the feasibility of appointing college students as advisers to boards of trustees, the Fairfax County Board of Supervisors appointed a high school student to the school board with full voting powers.

A turn-around in attitude began when the General Assembly toured Northern Virginia in 1960 as the guests of Fairfax, Falls Church, Arlington, and Alexandria.

Then Virginia cities in the urban corridor began to experience some of the pangs that had beset their brethren to the north. They felt a growing respect for the pioneers on the New Frontier.

Potomac River dashes over rocks in Great Falls Park

Beautiful Great Falls lies within 15 miles of the White House. Potomac River, cascading over huge boulders, drops 77 feet in less than three-quarters of a mile and plunges noisily into rugged Mather Gorge. Sightseers may follow trails in 800 acres of woods and swamp and view abandoned locks in the Potomac River Canal.

And as Northern Virginia became more crowded – 40 per cent of Arlington's population lived in apartments by 1970 – the residents began to appreciate the unhurried style in communities to the south. It was a time of mutual discovery.

Virginians became aware that Northern Virginia was an area of incredible diversity, a mixture of the cosmopolitan and the Ruritan.

It is the country of Metro, the rapid rail transit system, 30 miles of track that by 1990 will be hauling 29,000 commuters every morning into Washington to work and 14,000 from the city to jobs in Virginia's suburbs.

It is the land of the braves, headquarters in Loudoun County for the Washington Redskins, the better, for one thing, to be near Dulles Airport.

Fabulous Dulles!, perhaps the world's most stunning airport, a flying carpet slung in the sky, a facility built for once with space projected beyond next week. Built at a cost of $109 million, called a white elephant by some critics, it has proved a stunning bargain.

Architect Eero Saarinen called his masterwork "unique because it is the first commercial airport really to be planned from the start for jet airplanes. I think this terminal building is the best thing I've done. I think it is going to be really good."

In five counties radiating from Dulles are a dozen packs of foxhounds with kennels, hunt staffs, and established hunting country. Their spokesmen appear before the State Highway Commission to protest the widening of two-lane roads between stone walls. Around Middleburg, Capitol of the Horse Country, are 80 thoroughbred horse farms. Horses from all over the country are sent to the Middleburg Training Center before making their debut on the track.

Northern Virginia is the site of the labyrinthian Pentagon that in 1943 collected military personnel from 17 buildings under one roof, the world's largest office structure, offering three times the floor space of the Empire State Building, with 15 miles of pneumatic tubing, and the myth of the Western Union boy who entered the maze one day and came out 10 years later a Colonel. But even the Pentagon couldn't house the proliferating military.

Only 15 miles from the White House is Great Falls Park, 800 acres where urban dwellers can roam in deep woods or through the gem of a 30-acre swamp, or stand at the end of the roaring falls, a long incline of a thundering torrent as the Potomac smashes past rocks. The effect is of the earth's splitting at the seams and geysering water in all directions. One's first thought is for a plumber.

Northern Virginia is the area of massive traffic. It requires the one-mile stretch of Interstate 95 near the Pentagon that cost more than $53 million, with two triple-deck interchanges, or mixing bowls, and 17 bridges. At one point, the various roadways stretch 27 lanes.

147

"You just shut your eyes and drive," advised a Northern Virginian. "You almost have to know what you want to do in Fairfax to get in the right lane in Arlington."

By contrast, there's Leesburg, the seat of Loudoun County, so quiet a visitor could hear a leaf drop in the street.

Nearby is Morven Park, the lavish estate left Virginians by independent-minded Governor Westmoreland Davis, who served from 1918 to 1922.

The Democratic Organization of his day would just as soon have dropped him through a memory hole, but the record is there: a workman's compensation act, centralized purchasing agency, executive state budget that became a model for other states, laws protecting minors and mothers.

Among newcomers that Governor Davis introduced into government were innovative Colonel Leroy Hodges and Violet McDougall, efficient secretary to four Governors until she moved to the Mansion as the wife of Governor Pollard.

"Westmoreland Davis loved to josh people," Mrs. Pollard remembered, "but he would treat anybody with straw in his hair as a special person because he felt that individual couldn't look after himself. But if a Richmond banker came in the office, Governor Davis put on his fighting clothes because he figured the banker was after something for himself. Westmoreland Davis was for the underdog." Now his home is open to all who care to come.

The Northern Virginia Regional Park Authority set an example for the rest of the State in harnessing local governments for developing regional parks, including 2,019 acres along Manassas, site of the first major Civil War Battle. There Stonewall Jackson earned his sobriquet. (South Carolina's General Bee, dying, tried to hearten his troops by calling, "There stands Jackson like a stone wall! Rally behind the Virginians!")

The statue of Jackson on Little Sorrel dominates the battlefield, as he did so many in his life. He was a mixture of tenderness and ferocity. In Lexington, he taught black children Sunday School, and, on leave during the war, cut out paperdolls for a little girl. In battle, when a Confederate officer chided his men for concentrating their fire on a gallant Union officer, Jackson said, "No, Captain, the men are right; kill the brave ones, they lead on the others."

Dying of wounds he had received accidentally from his own troops after the triumph at Chancellorsville, Jackson, in delirium, uttered one of warfare's most memorable lines: "Let us cross over the river and rest in the shade of the trees." Bruce Catton and other historians have pointed out that they were not words of quiet resignation. It was an order, coupled with the promise of some shade, as one cajoles a

Stonewall loom over Manassas Battlefield Park

A peaceful park and now prevails where North and South grappled in their first major battle of the Civil War and where Thomas J. Jackson earned his nickname. Both sides learned that the struggle would be a long and bloody conflict.

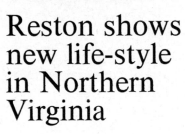

Reston shows new life-style in Northern Virginia

Each weekend in Reston the community's ar ists and craftsmen offer their work for sale at market in the plaza. Meanwhile, others, who ar so minded, swim or sail on Lake Anne, Life in the first completely planned town in the Unitec States seems to be going smoothly. The idea

isn't brand new. In
1484, Leonardo da Vinci
proposed 10 satellite
cities to relieve heavy over-
crowding in plague-
stricken Milan. In fact, in
moving from the city to the
green suburbs, nearly
every American is looking
for an uncluttered
life. But Reston marked the
first effort at testing the

concept. Apparently,
it is working. By 1972 Reston's population had
exceeded 16,000, with ex-
pectations of reach-
ing its full projected growth
of 75,000 persons
by 1980. The campus-like
community of Reston
is drawing such esteemed
firms as the National
Education Association.

Reston's main plaza has air of worlds fair

In totally planned Reston some 45 per cent of the space is supposed to be set aside for public purposes: schools, parks, lakes, roads, trails, churches, golf courses, swimming pools, tennis courts, walkways, and ample open areas. In compliance with the pla Gulf Reston turned over $700,000 worth of re creational facilities in 1971 to the Reston Home owners Association. On special routes, children can walk to school, play.

child, to get one more step out of his weary foot-cavalry and get in a good position for the next day's fighting, thinking until his pulse stopped about coming to grips with the enemy.

Near Dulles is Reston, the first major effort in the United States to plan and build at one fell swoop a full-scale, self-contained city on the perimeter of a larger urban center. In seven goals that Robert Simon set down for building Reston (a name formed from his initials) the first was that "the widest choice of opportunities be made available for the full use of leisure time." And entering the original unit, Lake Anne Village, with the 15-story Heron House rising above 30-acre Lake Anne, like a sprout breaking out of a bulb, the immediate feeling is of being part of a festival, or on a Worlds Fair set.

And if there is a new town of Reston, there is the Old Town of Alexandria, with Christ Church, where George Washington had his pew, and the Friendship Fire Company, a volunteer corps, to which he contributed an engine, it's said. There is Captain's Row, early homes of sea captains built when Alexandria's port was thriving. "The Alexandrians," observed one of them, "are in love with their houses. They stand around at parties and while other people are discussing their cars or children, they talk about what they're doing in the way of restoration. They're all home-oriented. They introduce somebody as being from such and such a place. In the rest of Virginia it may be who you are; in Alexandria, it's where you are. Mostly the work has been done by individuals and foundations, no one major corporation. The citizens are very zealous about going to City Council to preserve the area from high-rise apartments and the like."

Alexandria manages to blend the old and the new. In redeveloping Market Square, the town officials left space for Alexandria's farmers market beside City Hall, to which shoppers repair every Saturday morning, as they have been doing for more than 200 years.

One feature that lends style to life in Northern Virginia is Wolf Trap Farm, 117 acres near Vienna, 17 miles from Washington in the tree-covered foothills of the Blue Ridge. It demonstrates how art can create a sense of spaciousness in an urban environment, room in which the spirit can roam, an experience equivalent to the liberated feeling of running along Virginia Beach or climbing Old Rag Mountain in the Blue Ridge. Art pushes back the walls.

Mrs. Jouett Shouse, Washington, D.C., art patron and heiress to the Filene department store fortune of Boston, gave the land and $2 million for the first national park dedicated to the performing arts.

In March, 1971 a fire caused $650,000 damage to the incomplete facilities. "We shouldn't be smiling, but we are," said Mrs. Shouse. "We are smiling at the prospect of rebuilding." It opened on schedule July 1.

The park's centerpiece, the Filene Center, named for Mrs. Shouse's parents, slants on a hillside. Constructed of Oregon cedar that weathers to a silvery gray, it seems a natural part of the setting.

The theater seats 3,500, but floor-to-ceiling louvers open to the out-of-doors and help direct sound to as many as 3,000 seated on the grass. The sweeping building is at once an auditorium and itself a musical instrument, a vast hand cupped to catch and guide the sound.

The stage – 100 feet wide, 64 feet deep, with a proscenium arch 28 feet high – can display the most elaborate opera or lavish musical. Typifying the loving attention given the structure's details is the mildew-resistant stage curtain. Its striped blue, brown, and orange cloth was hand-woven of mohair and nylon by 126 craftsmen working six months in Swaziland, Africa.

Part of the project is the Wolf Trap American University Academy for the Performing Arts which grants scholarships to youths in every state for summer work in orchestra and chorus. The Park also sponsors a resident musical theater company. Wolf Trap's taste in a summer's offerings was indicated by the inaugural program, a concert by the National Symphony Orchestra with Van Cliburn.

To attend a program at Wolf Trap is pretty nearly the perfect way to take culture. A devotee of a particular medium can sit inside, near the performers, so as not to miss a note. On the other hand, the less than devoted feels no constraint to prop himself up in a seat inside but can wander outside and recline on the grass – much more aesthetic this way, he murmurs to his companion – look at the stars, watch the others who are less than connoisseurs, and probably hear more than if he were cooped up inside while his mind wandered. It is a question of taking or leaving art but deriving the most from it either way.

Crowning the slope of Arlington National Cemetery is a stuccoed mansion spreading 140 feet across the front, with a deep portico upheld by eight massive doric columns, called variously the Lee Mansion, the Custis Mansion, and Arlington House. It looks out on the District of Columbia, a view that Lafayette called the finest in America. This was the view that faced Robert E. Lee as he struggled over an offer to lead the Union forces against the South and Virginia.

George Washington Parke Custis, adopted son of George Washington and the grandson of Martha Washington by her first marriage, built the mansion. His daughter, Mary, married Lee in the great house. They lived and reared their children there 30 years until in 1861 Lee paced and prayed and went to his desk and wrote his resignation from the Army.

After they left Arlington, Mrs. Lee tried to pay taxes on the property to keep the title clear, but tax officials refused to accept a payment because it was not made in person. At a sale the government took

Viewing bright Dulles at night

Is it a bird?
Is it a hammock slung
in the sky?
Is it a slide?
Is it a board
from which to dive?
Is it a slope
to try, or is it
a carpet on which to fly?
Is it a wing,
or simply the rush
of air going by?

155

title to the land for $26,800. The Lees' son Custis contested the sale after the war, and the U.S. Supreme Court ruled in his favor. By then the estate had become a cemetery and Lee sold it to the government for $150,000.

No other cemetery can compare to Arlington. The list of persons buried there is an index to the Nation's history. But the most renown tomb is to the Unknown Soldier. After four major wars Americans are still drawn to the massive marble tomb of the World War I soldier and the graves of the World War II and Korean unknown soldiers placed in the plaza just in front of the World War I memorial.

The Nation seems to have been at war interminably, but the people, nearly two million a year, still come to view the tombs. They stand silently and look at the flawlessly hewn block of marble, the austere rectangle with the white purity of sacrifice, a memorial not to just a single unknown American but to all the servicemen who died. They stare at the white marble block, and the only break in the silence is the tread of the sentries, the clap of white-gloved hands on brown gun-stock, the click of heels. Who is not unknown, except to a handful? Those who are left come and look at marble blocks and the white markers on the green hillside, so numerous that the precise lines blur to a haze. They think of the sacrifice of so many and feel a shared loss.

Usually they visit the memorials to President John F. Kennedy and his brother Robert. On the President's grave is a stone, five feet in diameter, found at Cape Cod, from which flickers a flame. Around the grave is a terrace and below the terrace an overlook of gray granite. Carved into the overlook's low slanting wall, like a child's school desk, are seven quotations from the President's Inaugural address, concluding:

> With good conscience our only sure reward
> with history the final judge of our deeds
> let us go forth to lead the land we love,
> asking His blessing and His help,
> but knowing that here on Earth
> God's work must truly be our own.

Let a woman get in Gunston Hall, and it practically takes a charge of dynamite to blast her out, and then she leaves reluctantly, vowing to return. George Mason, who built it for his 16-year-old bride, Ann Eilbeck of Maryland, was even more reluctant to leave it. He was frequently absent from public meetings during the Revolutionary era and nearly always late, and no wonder seeing the home he had left behind. Nothing in Williamsburg could compensate for his own roof overlooking the Potomac. Mason was a man who liked every detail correct in a state paper or a dwelling, and he had William Buckland, a craftsman from England, work three years on the finishing touches at Gunston Hall, down to the carved pendant pine cone, the symbol of hospitality, hung in the double arched hallway.

The gardens are equally elegant, with boxwood bushes standing 12 to 14 feet high and extending 200 feet toward the broad, blue Potomac. No other plant enchants women more than the box, or bawx. It is the aristocrat of shrubs or trees, decorous, a well-behaved, willing clump, easily managed, and pruned into whatever shape is desired. Further, the boxwood has a pungent, subtle scent that once sniffed tantalizes ever after as one ponders what it resembles. Colonial housewives used to spread newly washed bed sheets on huge boxwood to dry.

Gunston Hall's most important room is the study and its most precious furnishing is a black-walnut table 20 inches wide and 30 inches long. Here George Mason wrote the Virginia Declaration of Rights, the basis for the United States Constitution's Bill of Rights.

He was an intensely private person forever being drawn into public life by contemporaries who appreciated his abilities. Service in public office, he said, was "an oppressive and unjust invasion of my personal liberty." Yet he always went, driven by his conscience, pulled by his friends.

He is a major figure of minor renown, which is the way he wished it during his lifetime. His tardiness arose not from any defect in character but a determination to live at his own pace. He understood lifestyle before the term originated. He loathed to leave his home and Ann. After she died at 39, he was left to be "father and mother to the poor orphans." (Mason made his will a few days after she died, and although he remarried seven years later, he wore mourning the rest of his life. Of Ann he wrote, "She never met me without a smile.")

When his neighbor and close friend, George Washington was elected Commander-in-Chief, Mason consented to take his place in the July convention of 1775 at Williamsburg. Later he wrote Washington: " I never was in so a disagreeable situation and almost dispaired of a cause which I so saw ill conducted ... Mere vexation and disgust threw me into such an ill state of health, that before the Convention rose, I was sometimes near fainting in the house. ... However, after some weeks the babblers were pretty well silenced, a few weighty members began to take the lead, several wholesome regulations were made."

Yet, despite his reluctance, Mason always was ready with words at the crucial moment. Virginia's last Colonial convention began on May 6, and Mason arrived on May 17, in time to propose guarantees for individual liberties and the Virginia Constitution to implement them.

Some of the reasoning in the Declaration of Rights was expressed a year earlier in a paper recommending annual election of officers of the Fairfax Company:

"We came equal into the world, and equal we shall go out of it. All men are by nature born equally free and independent.... Every society, all government,

To get away from it all, go to Wolf Trap Farm, the first national park to be dedicated to the performing arts, and one also of the few theaters where the viewer may sit outside and still be accounted among those on the inside. The stage is vast, some 64 feet deep, 100 feet wide, 24 feet high, or if the viewer is sitting outside, even vaster. The limit is the sky.

Wolf Trap Farm features indoor outdoor theater

A constant procession views President Kennedy's memorial in Arlington National Cemetery. Nearby, flowers mark Robert Kennedy's grave. The guard changes at the Tomb of the Unknown Soldier. Overlooking the cemetery is Arlington House, built by George Custis, whose daughter Mary married Robert E. Lee. The Lees left Arlington in 1861 and never returned. The estate was made into a cemetery.

Arlington draws many visitors to honor heroes

and every kind of civil compact, is or ought to be calculated for the general good and safety of the community. ... And whenever any power or authority extends further, or is in larger duration than is in its nature necessary for the purposes, it may be called government, but it is in fact oppression.

"In all our associations, in all our agreements, let us never lose sight of this fundamental maxim — that all power was originally lodged in and consequently is derived from the people. We should wear it as a breastplate and buckle it on as an armour."

Mason never took off the armour. As a delegate to the Federal Convention he declined to sign the Constitution because it embraced the compromise between New England and the deep South on the tariff and slave trade. His final words at the Richmond convention on the Constitution were directed against slave trade as "diabolical in itself and disgraceful to mankind."

Mason and Washington were nearly as much a team as Jefferson and Madison. Once, Washington asked him, "Mr. Mason, what services in the power of the people can I bestow on you?"

"Your services as President of the United States, Mr. Washington," Mason replied.

Everywhere the visitor turns in Fredericksburg he finds George Washington, beginning at Ferry Farm, where, Parson Weems said, George chopped down his father's favorite cherry tree and threw a Spanish dollar across the Rappahannock River. "The place of my growing infancy," Washington called the town.

All his life it was a second home. His youngest brother Charles built and operated the Rising Sun Tavern, a favorite gathering place for Virginia patriots. Surgeon Hugh Mercer, an old comrade from the French and Indian War, kept an apothecary shop. Washington, while visiting the town, kept his books in Mercer's sitting room.

Washington's sister, Betsy, had a lovely plantation home, Kenmore. Her husband, Fielding Lewis, was armorer of the Revolution. At the request of the Virginia Committee of 1775, he ran the Manufactory of Small Arms, outfitted ships, and supervised care of sick and wounded soldiers. He also ran himself deep in debt advancing money for the factory and ruined his health. He was that rarity, a bankrupt munitions maker. He died not long after the British surrender at Yorktown. Over the years Betty Lewis had to sell the plantation piece by piece. Finally, she gave up the house itself and went to live with a daughter in Culpeper.

At the foot of Kenmore's garden is the cottage George built for his mother Mary. He was a dutiful son. Indeed, her stringent demands probably account as much as any one influence for Washington's sense of duty. He addressed her as "Honored Madam" in his letters.

Gardening was her chief pleasure, and the Garden Clubs of Virginia have restored her beds and borders to a degree that probably would satisfy even her critical eye.

In the midst of the war a mud-spattered courier came riding to the garden, trailed by a crowd eager for news from the front. Mary Washington finished digging up some plant or other for a neighbor, wiped her hands deliberately, broke open the seal, read, and digested it, and finally announced to the impatient townspeople, "George has crossed the Delaware."

At least that's the story they tell in Fredericksburg.

On the way from New York to Philadelphia in November, 1781, George stopped with his staff in Fredericksburg. At a reception Mary entered the hall leaning on his arm. If such were the mothers of America, exclaimed the gallant French officers, "no wonder the sons were so illustrious." Lafayette paying her a visit in the garden was moved to murmur, going away, that he had met the only Roman matron of the day. George discouraged the matriarch from visiting Mount Vernon and his compliant Martha. Apparently some differences of temperament were too great for even the father of his country to try to reconcile.

An obelisk, a miniature of the Washington Monument, has been erected by the women of America to "Mary, Mother of George." On a hillside nearby is Meditation Rock, where Mary, it is said, read to her grandchildren.

Walking through the high-ceilinged rooms at Kenmore, visitors marvel at the gracious style of life the Lewises and their 11 children enjoyed before he sank his fortune and his health in the Revolution. The arms factory is gone, but near the site Gunnery Spring still flows. A legend, kept fresh by the Fredericksburg Information Center, declares: "He who drinks of the spring, no matter where he may wander, will certainly come back to Fredericksburg." Washington did, anyway.

Among other attractions is the office where James Monroe began in 1786 his long public carrier. It has the desk, with secret compartments, on which he signed the Monroe Doctrine. Another stop, Stoner's Museum, is outfitted as a 19th century general store, pot-belly stove, cracker barrel, and a string of peppers from the ceiling. In some remote areas of Virginia, one can still come upon the real thing.

In Virginia is a land, fairer than day, known as the Northern Neck, a peninsula between the Potomac and Rappahannock rivers. The Neck's western boundary is debatable, but one version has the line running from the falls of the Rappahannock at Fredericksburg to the falls of Aquia Creek, just north of Fredericksburg.

The Northern Neck is full of good food harvested from the land and the rivers and creeks, but the most noted crop is famous men, as well as the women who bore the children. And the most intensely cultivated plot is the estate of Stratford, homeplace of the Lees.

George Mason's elegant Gunston Hall overlooks lovely garden

In exquisite Gunston Hall is a small table. Here patriot George Mason wrote the Declaration of Rights. He attended to details, whether in the superb carving of his little mansion or splendid phrasing in a document. The gardens show some of Virginia's best boxwood. Nearby is Woodlawn, home of George Washington's nephew, Lawrence Lewis, and Nelly Custis, Martha Washington's grandchild.

Trees frame Mount Vernon on river bluff

Mount Vernon, America's best known home, draws thousands through its doors. George Washington inherited the farmhouse from his brother Lawrence and enlarged it by adding a third story providing six bedrooms and planning additions to the ends. In the entrance hall hangs the key to the Bastile, given to Washington by his old comrade, Lafayette.

A visit to Mount Vernon closes at the crypt where George and Martha Washington are buried. In picture at right is the site of George Washington's birthplace at rural Wakefield in Westmoreland County, where he lived until he was three. The original house, built by his father, burned to the ground during the Revolutionary War. A memorial mansion, typical of the period, has been built on the old foundations. The air, the lay of the land and the look of the water, and the surrounding forests need no reconstruction.

Visitors revere Washington's Tomb at Mount Vernon

Fredericksburg stakes claim as "State's most historic city"

Stoner's Museum, left, deals exclusively in nostalgia in its guise as a 19th century general store. In a long story-and-a-half building, upper right, James Monroe began practicing law. His office contains the desk on which Monroe composed the message enunciating his Doctrine; the dispatch box he used while negotiating the Louisiana Purchase, and his Revolutionary gun. The Rising Sun Tavern, lower right, was the scene for rising patriotic sentiment against the British crown. Charles Washington, George's brother, built the tavern. Here Jefferson, Mason, Wythe, Pendleton, and Thomas Lee met to begin revising Virginia laws.

The first thing to notice about Stratford is that it was built to last, with brick walls two feet thick standing directly on the ground as if the house simply grew there, a house designed as a bulwark against Indians, wars, and time itself. It lacks the teasing subtleties of Monticello, the stateliness of Westover, or the benignity of Mount Vernon, but it has a satisfying sturdiness.

Splendidly symmetrical, the house, as if it is meant to carry out the first letter in House on an ABC block, is built in an H. The two wings, each 60 feet long and 30 feet wide, form the uprights of the H, like goal posts, and the central hall, measuring 30 by 30 feet, is the cross bar. From each end of the house rises a group of four chimney stacks joined by arches forming pavilions above the rooftops. The great hall opens directly onto a flight of stairs leading down to the lawn. Outside, at each corner of the house is a dependency – school house, lumber house, law office, and a kitchen with a fireplace big enough to roast an ox. Nearby was the grist mill, sawmill, and wharf. Life here was set solidly, made four-square and self-sufficient.

Down the fan-shaped steps came four generations of Lees, a host of public servants, including 12 members of the House of Burgesses, four Governors, and two signers of the Declaration of Independence. Thomas Lee, who began building the house about 1725, was a Burgess who in time became President of His Majesty's Council. Two of his sons, Richard Henry and Francis Lightfoot Lee, signed the Declaration of Independence. Two other sons, Arthur and William Lee, represented the United States abroad as diplomats.

"A band of brothers," John Adams said of them, "intrepid and unchangeable, who like the Greeks at Thermopylae stood in the gap, in the defence of their country from the first glimmering of the Revolution in the horizon, through all its rising light to its perfect day."

In the line was Light Horse Harry Lee, Washington's cavalry leader who, as a Congressman, eulogized his commander as "first in war . . . peace . . . and the heart of his country." His son, born at Stratford, was Robert E. Lee, who was connected in one way or another, it seems, with every major plantation in Virginia, but spent most of his life in the saddle.

The most famous area of the house is the "mother's room," where the Lee women gave birth to their numerous distinguished offspring. The builder's wife, Hannah, had nine.

One should not leave the Neck's creeks and estuaries without some words about the marshes arrayed around the year in subtle, shifting shades from beige to deep brown, and pale yellow to flaming green and bright gold, as if they are endlessly changing on Nature's loom, weaving before your eyes.

The mass of the world has come to appreciate a marsh only lately, anyway. For too long a marsh was

Stratford Hall, home of Lees, rises above Potomac River

Thomas Lee completed massive old Stratford about 1732 in Westmoreland County. In the H-shaped house, the huge center hall is 30-foot square. A spacious kitchen has a fireplace fit for an ox. From the hall issued a host of great men, including two brothers, Thomas Henry and Francis Lightfoot Lee, who signed the Declaration of Independence. Robert E. Lee was born at Stratford and dreamed of returning one day to the broad ancestral estate.

Blue Ridge Hunt sets out near Millwood

*Elegantly attired hunters
and eager hounds
set out from Carter Hall estate: in search of the
fox. The pillared mansion,
constructed in 1792,
served as Stonewall Jack-
son's headquarters
and John Mosby's hideout.
Middleburg and
Warrenton are regarded as
capitals for foxhunting.
The jets' whine at Dulles
mingles in Loudoun County
with the pack's chorus.*

regarded as something merely to be tolerated at best and filled in as quickly as possible, an embarrassment to be got out of the way as the housewife tidies a mess. But the marsh even in drear winter dress is a vast brown bed of productivity, the sea's pantry, the beginning of the food chain, creating minute organisms that support life in the ocean. It all starts in the marshes.

There are moreover, aside from the economics of the seafood industry on which one must base a plea to legislators to save the marshes, the aesthetics, the pleasure of watching a marsh change under the sun, rain, and seasons.

The creek or river winds through the brown bed to the horizon, leading the eye around bends and coves, even more enticing in some ways than an open expanse of water, without the sinuous path drawing the eye this way and that. To follow the line of the creek through the mat of marsh grass is like studying a jigsaw puzzle and finding endlessly changing patterns and pieces.

Which is the more exciting, marshes or mountains? The marsh bending under the wind, or the mountain with cloud patterns moving slowly over it, a leopard changing its spots before your eyes?

The mountains inspire contemplation, the marshes investigation. The mountains, massive and monumental, suggest acceptance; the marshes, shifting and waving, stir curiosity. What's going on down there? Who's moving around? It is where life began and is beginning, and it is what sustained life so long. The man in the boat, messing around, feels he is in touch with the elemental, the muck.

The marshes suggest beginnings, the mountains conclusions, the marshes stimulate activity, the mountains induce repose. The marsh and the sea say go, the mountain advises abide. The marsh and the sea are life and the mountains are old time. The mountain makes the viewer wish to rest on a rock and look over a vista, the marshes urge him to get in a boat and push off. It is a never-ending debate, the marsh or the mountain, and need not be settled in Virginia, which has a capacious supply of both. Some Virginians, especially those in the middle in the piedmont, split their vacations three ways – a week in the marsh, a week in the mountains, and a week at home.

For the vacationer in Northern Neck one of the amenities is an unlimited supply of crabs. There's something peculiarly satisfying about crabbing. All a person needs is a piece of string with bait (generally, chicken necks or backs), a net, and a basket or pail in which to put the catch. With crab meat hovering around $3 a pound in stores, to wade near the shore and scoop a Chesapeake Blue Shell Crab in a net is as easy and rewarding as picking up money in a dream.

Further, the crab is delicious. Among a variety of ways to prepare crabs for the table, all good, a common one is to steam them 30 minutes in a pot

containing a little water, a half cup of vinegar (some çooks also add a cup of beer), and a dash of cayenne pepper. The diner removes the shell, which turned red during the steaming, picks out the light, white meat, and dips the bits into melted butter or sauce with a mayonnaise or tomato base. There is no limit to the crabs one can catch or eat.

George Washington was born in the Northern Neck at Wakefield, a plantation overlooking the Potomac River. He lived there until he was three and the family moved 50 miles up the Potomac to Hunting Creek Plantation, now known as Mount Vernon.

Wakefield accidentally burned to the ground during the Revolution, and the family abandoned the site. Just before Washington's 200th birthday, Congress authorized funds, and a memorial mansion typical of the period was built on the old foundations. As a youth Washington returned to his birthplace to visit relatives and to hunt, fish, and, surely, to crab.

Mount Vernon is the most widely revered of American homes. Even those who know few details of George Washington's life sense his integrity and come to pay homage to his memory. The line of visitors, winding from the rear of the great house, across the vast lawn, and down the hillside to buses and cars could be a demographic picture – all size, shapes, ages, races, and incomes – of the United States. At times the whole Nation seems bent on tramping through the house. In the back of nearly everybody's mind is the thought that one day one must go through Mount Vernon.

From Mount Vernon, Washington wrote an English correspondent, "No estate in United America is more pleasantly situated than this." The view across the board, blue Potomac is beguiling. Land on other plantations, however, was far more fertile. Washington struggled with it all his life to make it productive. As to the house, it verges on being jerry-built, growing, like so many American farmhouses, with the owner's needs.

Washington inherited Mount Vernon from his older half-brother, Lawrence, and there he brought his bride, Martha Dandridge Custis, a wealthy widow with two children. He expanded the estate from 2,126 to 8,000 acres and changed Mount Vernon by adding an additional story and extending it north and south. The windows in the second story are almost lost from view under the portico.

Yet, being Washington's, Mount Vernon, serene, is immune from strictures. The gleaming white-pillared mansion with the pink roof and sprightly cupola, spreading across the brow of the green bluff above the blue Potomac, has a shimmering, almost evanescent appearance, partly because the walls' wood slabs edges have been beveled to look like blocks of icy white stone.

And, of course, the house is mixed inextricably in the minds of the beholders with Washington and their

Virginia looks across Potoma at District of Columbia

The view over the Potoma is calm, serene. The Washington Monument's slender spire would tie, it seems, earth to heaven. Beneath the spire march the Lincoln Memorial's noble columns. Beyond rises the Capitol. Jefferson, Madison, Washington, the Virginian wanted it there, horse-traded with Alexander Hamilton to take it away from Philadelphia, s they could keep close watch. It was a good swap

Heroic statuary of flag raisers dwarfs viewers

An enlargement in bronze of Joe Rosenthal's famous photograph depicts Marines raising the Stars and Stripes on Iwo Jima's Mount Surabachi on February 23, 1945. Figures tower 30 feet and the flag pole 60 feet. On base is Admiral Nimitz's tribute: "Uncommon valor was a common virtue."

175

own childhoods at Washington Birthday Parties and tiny toy hatchets with dark blue handles, red heads, and silver-white edges. When visitors look at Mount Vernon they see the Father of His Country, either in resplendent dress and powdered white wig or in his blue and buff uniform, waving a cocked hat, astride a white charger. Or they see portrait hanging above the classroom blackboard, a prim, pink sphinx as painted by Gilbert Stuart.

His distinguishing traits were an absolutely unimpeachable integrity, the sense of judgment that marked so many of the founders, and a tremendous holding power. During the war when his army had shrunk to 3,000 ragged men against 30,000 British, Washington said that if defeated, he would gather what few he could and withdraw to the wilderness of Augusta County, and if beaten there, he would fall back beyond the Alleghenies, but never give up.

He was trained in adversity. A young Colonel, he was with General Edward Braddock when the Britisher was wounded fatally trying to take Fort Duquesne from the French and Indians. Braddock had five horses shot from under him. Washington had two horses shot. Four bullets pierced his clothing. Dying, Braddock praised the Colonial troops, and of the French and Indians said, "You shall better know how to deal with them another time."

In the other times, facing vastly superior British forces, Washington's strategy most of the way, while he tried to put together and train an army, was never to let the enemy catch him head-on in conflict on the open field.

The local militia waxed and waned with the seasons, Congress vacillated when Washington pleaded for supplies, and at times he alone seemed to be bearing the burden of the Revolution. In the terrible December of 1777, "you might have tracked the army from White Marsh to Valley Forge by the blood of their feet," Washington said At Valley Forge he went to ground and had his men build huts. Nearly 3,000 died of hunger and cold. Baron von Steuben observed that no European army would have held together under such hardships. But the troops and the people had faith in Washington.

Over and over in desperate situations, as when the Continentals were being routed during the Battle of Monmouth, Washington, oblivious to the hail of musket balls, would appear, almost an apparition on his huge white horse, and electrify and rally his men. Lafayette left a picture of him at such a moment: "His presence stopped the retreat. His fine appearance on horseback, his calm courage, raised to animation by the vexations of the morning, gave him the air best calculated to excite enthusiasm. He rode all along the lines amid the shots of the soldiers, cheering them by his voice and example and restoring to our standard the fortunes of the fight. I thought then, as now, that never had I beheld so superb a man."

Washington had a way of bringing out the best in men. They tried to live up to his expectations. After

the war, as Congress delayed paying the army, some officers circulated anonymous papers hinting at mutiny.

Washington was well aware of the sentiments. "This Army," he wrote a friend, "is of near eight years' standing, six of which has been spent in the field without any other shelter from the inclemency of the seasons except that of tents or such houses as they could build for themselves... They have encountered hunger, cold and nakedness. They have fought many battles and bled freely. They have lived without pay... Are they to be turned adrift soured and discontented, complaining of the ingratitude of their country?..."

But rather than yield to any dishonorable plan, Washington, as his aide Alexander Hamilton noted, "would sooner suffer himself to be cut to pieces."

The General issued an order for his officers to meet March 15, 1783. He denounced the hint of mutiny and promised they could freely command his services in attaining "complete justice for all your toils and dangers." Do not, he urged, take "any measure which, viewed in the calm light of reason, will lessen the dignity and sully the glory you have hitherto maintained..."

Then an unexpected bit of byplay melted the hearts of the men. Washington began to read to them a letter from a Virginia Congressman explaining the financial problems with which Congress was struggling. The better to read it, he paused to take his new spectacles from his pocket, and, putting them on, he looked at his officers and said, "Gentlemen, you must pardon me. I have grown gray in your service and now find myself growing blind."

In his own day people saw him as if with the eyes of posterity. In the last stage of the war, when he and his staff were en route to Williamsburg, they stopped at a farm house for breakfast. An old man from the neighborhood entered the room, stood and fixed his eyes on Washington's face, and continued staring until the officers quieted their conversation and watched. In the stillness the old man, looking upward, said, "Lord now lettest thou thy servant depart in peace, for mine eyes have seen thy salvation."

During Washington's Presidency, the brilliant contentious young men in his administration continued to turn to him as a fountainhead of judgment In concluding a lengthy plea to Washington to run for a second term, Jefferson wrote:

"The confidence of the whole union is centered in you. Your being at the helm will be more than an answer to every argument which can be used to alarm and lead the people in any quarter into violence and secession. North and South will hang together if they have you to hang on."

And in our own time, a Mount Vernon women's political club, responding to down-state criticisms of their area, issued automobile bumper stickers proclaiming: GEORGE WASHINGTON WAS A NORTHERN VIRGINIAN.

On the Shore

Consider Virginia's Eastern Shore, a 70-mile long peninsula lapped on one side by the Chesapeake Bay, on the other by the Atlantic Ocean, and threaded by thousands of creeks.

It's Virginia's market basket, producing 65 kinds of vegetables and fruits. Along Route 13, which runs up the peninsula to Maryland, every open inch is cultivated, a field of spring kale reaching all the way up to a family burial ground where four white headstones poke above the dark-green leafy sea.

Where roads branch off Route 13, signs tease the eye: Temperanceville, where four landowners sold acreage for the town on condition that it be forever dry; Modest Town, where two prim ladies kept a proper boarding house at a stage stop; Birdsnest, named for a tiny room cupped in a three-story building. Indian names also abound.

There are Assateague, stony river; Chincoteague, beautiful land across the water; Pungoteague, sand fly river. There are, as well, Nassawaddox, a stream between two streams; Assowoman, rock cave; Wachapreague, little city by the sea, Machapungo, much dust, and Onancock, foggy place.

All are worth following to quiet towns. The visitor may visit the site of Arlington, ancestral estate for which George Washington Parke Custis named the more celebrated Arlington in Northern Virginia. (Everything connects, eventually, in Virginia.)

In the family graveyard is the grave of John Custis IV, who died "Aged 71 years/and Yet liv'd but Seven Years which/was the space of time He kept a Batchelers/house at Arlington on the Eastern Shore/of Virginia."

Colonel Custis couldn't resist that final slam at his wife, Frances, daughter of Daniel Parke, governor of the Leeward Islands.

They were well-matched. From leading families, they were wealthy, strong-willed, and hot-tempered. Their marriage quickly settled into a perpetual quarrel. At last they decided not to speak at all, except through a slave, Pompey. Then, thinking, perhaps of a reconciliation, Colonel Custis invited his wife for a carriage drive, but, after riding a short distance across the hard-packed sand, he turned the horse sharp right and drove straight ahead into Chesapeake Bay.

When water was flowing over the floorboard, Frances asked: "Where are you going, Colonel Custis?"

"To hell, madam," he retorted.

"Drive on," she said, "any place is better than Arlington."

He turned the carriage to shore, and, driving home, he remarked, "Madam, I believe you would as lief meet the Devil himself if I should drive to hell."

"Quite true, Sir," she said. "I know you so well I would not be afraid to go anywhere you would go."

The visitor soon notices a distinctive kind of architecture on the Shore: a house with three or more levels of rooflines: a main house, hooked to a smaller box-like addition, and joined, generally, by a colonnade or breezeway to the third, smallest unit, a profile, perhaps of family growth. Sometimes, though, the final structure will burgeon nearly as large as the first, with the whole taking the shape of a crude wood block, saved from the saw for a toy.

Shore historian Henry A. Wise theorized that a tax on two-story houses in Colonial days prompted families to make only a portion at that height. The habit stuck.

On the ocean side of the shore is a chain of barrier islands. The two largest islands are Assateague, a national park, and nearby Chincoteague. During the last week in July Chincoteague's crabbers, oystermen, and fishermen put on high rubber boots to take part in the oldest continuous roundup in the Western Hemisphere.

Ponies swim across the channel to Chincoteague Island from their range on neighboring Assateague Island. Eager sce

into the water to watch the start of the annual roundup and auction in late July on Virginia's beautiful eastern shore.

After swimming channel, ponies rest, above, to catch their breath in a pasture. Then cowboys-for-a-day drive the ponies clattering through town and to the carnival grounds. There the ponies wait in a corral and customers look them over with an eye to the next day's auction. Nobody knows when or how the ponies came to live on sea-girt Assateague Island.

Watermen herd ponies along the main street

Auction profits help support fire department

At auction ponies go to the highest bidder at prices that range from $50 to $75. Young cowboy, below, introduces dappled pony to prospective young bidder. Humane society representatives follow annual roundup carefully to protect the horses and colts. After the auction, the cowboys herd older mares and stallions to the water's edge for the swim back across the

182

channel to Assateague, where the ponies will enjoy another year of roaming in the national park, protected by rangers, living amid ducks and geese on the barrier island. Most widely held theory is that ponies swam ashore when a Spanish ship wrecked in the 1550s. Auctions began in the 1920s, after two disastrous fires burned Chincoteague. The ponies came to the rescue.

Into L. L. Burton's ware-
house on Chincoteague
come 80 million clams
a year. From there they are
shipped by truck as far as
Miami, San Francisco,
and Canada. Other, smaller
distributors supply areas
closer by. In the wharf-side
warehouse men sort
a just-arrived shipment
of clams. In pictures above,
clam diggers guide boat
to flats. There they trace
clams by signs and dig them
with rakes. Chincoteague
is celebrated for its chowder
made with potatoes,
onions, tomatoes, and clams.

Chincoteague supplies clams for the Nation

Fires destroyed much of the town in 1922 and 1924. To raise funds for equipment the Chincoteague Volunteer Fire Department began holding an annual carnival and then to auctioning off ponies brought from Assateague. Nobody knows when the ponies came to Assateague. Ask a 'teaguer, and he will shrug his shoulders and say, "It was long before moi toime."

One theory is that the horses swam ashore from a Spanish galleon that shipwrecked in the 16th century. Some say settlers hid their steeds on Assateague in 1662 to escape a tax on horses. At any rate, Chincoteague residents always have kept horses on Assateague, and sheep as well in other times. Long before the carnival, so far back nobody can remember when the custom began, Chincoteaguers sailed and rowed to the neighboring island annually to pen the cattle and shear the sheep. Grubbing on the island's harsh fare, plus inbreeding, reduced the horses to a size somewhere between the pony and the ordinary horse. It is a medium-compact horse.

Two days prior to the swim the firemen go to Assateague and round up the ponies in a corral. Then, at low tide, they herd them to the marsh's edge, and wranglers in boats steer the herd across the narrow strait, where thousands of spectators line the shore to watch.

The crossing takes half an hour. Then, after a breathing spell, the cow punchers, with a good deal of whooping and arm-waving, drive the horses pell-mell along Chincoteague's main street to the corral on the carnival grounds. To those watching, it is somewhat like being caught in the midst of Rosa Bonheur's horse fair, as the galloping, mane-tossing, snorting, dappled tide of white, brown, black, and caramel ponies sweeps past the waterfront's neat white houses.

Next day they are auctioned off at prices ranging from $25 to $75 apiece. The humane society's representatives ride herd over the event to see that the cowboys-for-a-day don't hurt the ponies.

The firemen comply with the humane society's regulations, but they are skeptical about the necessity of them. One veteran wrangler observed that the humane society "people don't understand about these ponies. They think you oughtn't to sell a colt off'n its mother until the baby is four months old. But if you leave the colt on its mother for four months in the summer, the heat, mosquitos, and floies and colt together will pull that mother down until it gets so poor that when fall comes, she can't come back and may die in the winter. Another thing, when you take them colts off Assateague where the floies and ticks are so thick – sometimes you pick a thousand ticks off one pony – it's like putting a pony in heaven to let a child have 'im and keep 'im in a stable and feed and care for 'im."

On a quieter note than the pony roundup is the Weekend of the Islands, held during April, when the Eastern Shoremen exhibit their handicraft, and demonstrate the art of carving birds and animals, their big brown hands shaping enough beasts and fowl to populate the whole Shore.

Then on the first Wednesday in May there is a gastronomic spectacle to match anything Virginia can produce in cuisine – the Eastern Shore Annual Seafood Festival.

Adam and Eve couldn't have fared better.

(On the Shore, they tell you, they eat that way all the time. The Festival is for the deprived mainlanders.)

Not only is everything done to delicate perfection; all is laid out so a body doesn't have to jostle and elbow his neighbor as at a trough. A dozen stalls, made of pine saplings and rough boards, are spread around a sea-meadow. Each stand offers a different dish. It is an outdoor buffet set over so vast an expanse that a person need not wait at any point. If a half-dozen spectators are mesmerized googoo-eyed, while cooks spoon oyster-fritter batter onto the griddle and lift out light, sizzling brown concoctions that seem to float toward the plate, an impatient man can step 50 feet farther to the booth dispensing crisp, succulent clams. Or he can drift, idly as a jellyfish, to the next stand and take clams fresh off the shells, or mosey to the raw oyster bar just beyond, for fresh oysters.

Another stall offers steamed clams with mugs of clam broth, wreathed in smoke, a thick brew, misty gray, that lifts the diner's spirits when he sips it, like an ocean swell.

A gourmet takes his heavily laden dish to one of 200 trestle-tables, each set with bowls of iced salads – chunks of radish, celery stalks, olives. Then with the murmur of happy people, sea breezes in the pines, and the sun smiling on the scene, he eats.

The clams come by the half-dozen in nylon net bags, which the diner tears open, and then takes a clam, scoops the morsel from the shell, dips it in a patty of butter or vinegar, and exults in the nut-sweet flavor.

Fast as he finishes one lot, somebody drops another bag at his plate. He has to keep eating for politeness' sake. A fellow can't be so crude as to stand up and bray across the meadow "Hey, don't bring no more of them clams over here. I've had enough!"

There also is fried eel, which has a sour-sweet flavor, between roast pork and fried chicken, those who eat it say.

They who have acquired a taste for eel – and short of being shipwrecked how could one be brought to acquire it? – stand around chewing eel ostentatiously, and exclaiming, Man, I never tasted better fried eel.

Nobody is as stuck up as a person who has learned to stomach something nobody else will touch, and can thereby affect a hearty superiority

Bridge-Tunnel strides across Chesapeake Bay

The Chesapeake Bay Bridge-Tunnel, like a huge articulated snake, winds 17.5 miles, shore to shore, across the Chesapeake Bay from Norfolk to Eastern Shore. The construction, financed by a $200 million bond issue, require. 37 months. Above, a ship steams through Thimble Shoals Channel near the center of the span. Below a picture shows the approach on Eastern Shore.

Eastern Shore and Tidewater abound in birds and boats on quiet inlets and lagoons

A familiar scene in Tidewater is a shoreline graced by snowy egrets and ducks. A huge tree, knee-deep in water, is a lure to fishermen looking for bass. Work boats are moored at a marina. Tidewater's creeks and rivers flow toward the Chesapeake Bay, which is the largest estuary in the eastern United States. With a shoreline 4,600 miles long, it's the world's greatest fishing hole.

188

and exclaim that boy, you haven't lived until you have eaten whatever it is that he has learned to eat.

The seabreeze whets the appetite, and in May there's enough of a nip in it to make one go back for cup after cup of steaming broth, the essence of the clams drawn from spigots at the bottom of the tanks in which they are steaming. The beverage comes as near being the sea itself as any could.

The Festival's origin in 1969 offers an example of the way a tradition begins in Virginia, one frequently spouting from another.

Leonard L. Burton, a Chincoteague businessman, and H. B. Rew, cashier at the Farmers Merchants Bank of Onley, were on their way home from a Wakefield shadplanking one April evening, "picking the bones out of our gums, still hungry, and also tarred from listening to politicians," said Burton, "and we decided to have a festival where we wouldn't let anybody make a speech, just eat."

Primarily, he said, they aimed to clear enough from ticket sales to invite members of the General Assembly, State officials, and politicians as their guests and win recognition for the Shore. Other regions have hosted legislative tours, but the Eastern Shore Chamber of Commerce is the first to do so annually and in such a way as to make the party self-supporting and have nearly $10,000 surplus to invest in other civic enterprises.

Burton had the place — Tom's Cove, a camp ground with ample room for the crowd. Through his business as the largest clam distributor on the East Coast he also had helpful contacts. The esteemed clam broth, for instance, is brewed by his business associates from Cleveland. Thus evolved the Festival.

The causeway from the Shore to Chincoteague is one of Virginia's most spectacular drives, across green marshes, brown mudflats, and blue channels, flecked with birds of all colors. Early in the morning the visitor sees an open area in the marsh, about the size of a drop-the-handkerchief circle, filled with snowy egrets on the rim and ducks bobbing in the middle.

For an explanation one goes to Roy Tolbert, whose work with the Delmarva Council (Delaware, Maryland, Virginia) has spread the word about the three states' peninsula. Tolbert introduces Tom Reed, who, although past 70, has a face as tan and unlined as hard-packed sand. He fits Jefferson's vision of a man at one with nature and his work.

Most of Reed's life has been as a munger, one who makes his living from the marsh and sea. Now the Federal government employs him to assist wildlife research teams. If the research team needs turtles for a blood sampling, Tom Reed knows where they are. He reads the woods, reeds, and waves as pages of a book.

His voice is the sort a person would expect to hear when putting a seashell to the ear, with a forthright sounding of the vowel "o" so that the weak and spindly pronoun "I" becomes a full-bodied, splendid "Oy," and thin insipid time becomes lusty "toime."

As to the birds congregating in the marsh hole, he notes that the green algae absorbs the oxygen in the pool during the night, "and the minnows stick their heads out of the water to breathe, and that's what those birds were doing in there. That's how nature's a-working."

He knows the birds by what they call themselves, as well as the book-names: the American bittern, "which is a whap, he says it when he flies, anybody can tell he's a whap" . . . the tall, angular, majestic big blue heron, is a "crankey;" the little green heron is "a skauk, that's his call;" the sanderling is the "surf bird," which runs swiftly on the sand "and follows the wave out — dip-dip-dip — bobbing its head for food, and then when the wave comes back, it takes off," and then there's "the willet — it says that plain, the willet does, especially if he sees an enemy around, you know . . ."

The enemy the willet can't see is the poison that seeps from pesticides into the marshes and the shorebirds' systems. The ospreys are almost gone, the black ducks, once so prolific, are dwindling, and the merganser's going. Last summer Tom Reed only saw one bald eagle.

"Human nature's funny," he says. "It wants to kill anything that gets in its way. But you can't get rid of all life's miseries. The people who cry the most over mosquitos are the ones who never get bit by one. They work in the house. Now weeds are the farmer's best friend, but you try to convince one of that. Weeds cover the earth. The earth is alive, just like we are, and a bare spot hurts. Nature covers it in no time. It hurts my feelings when I see them using weed killer on the roadsides. They're working against nature when they do it."

He describes the work of a munger digging clams with his feet: "We wore clamming clothes — old clothes that we wore out in the winter, a blue flannel shirt, real warm, next to the body and an oilskin coat and linen moccasins, and you'd curl your foot around the clam, with a dab of mud and then — quick! — with the pressure of the water and the mud, you'd rake it up, legging 'em we called it. When the water's deeper, you hold the clam between your feet, bear your weight on the boat, and you jump and catch 'em.

"It was hard. A lot of times I dreaded to go in the cold, but it was a rewarding loif, it seems to me like, and I believe if I had to live my loif over again, I'd like to do the same thing."

Once separate, Eastern Shore now is connected to Virginia by the Chesapeake Bay Bridge-Tunnel.

The Shore is within four hours of a third of the Nation's population, 65 million people. As, increasingly, they come looking for refreshment, the question is whether they will extinguish or respect Tom Reed's whaps, crankeys, willets, and skauks.

Ships to build

Newport News is the Newport News Shipbuilding and Dry Dock Company.

Of course, its identity also is shaped by others, including Fort Eustis, the home of the U.S. Army Transportation Center, Tidewater's largest military post.

But mention Newport News, and most Virginians think first of the Shipyard, which was there first.

To them, Newport News is a welder in a blue shirt and a hard hat.

The Yard is Virginia's largest private employer. Its work force averages 17,000, and, when necessary, expands like an accordion to 28,000, drawing personnel from Eastern North Carolina.

In Carolina they used to call Newport News "Shipyard, Virginia."

Newport News probably was named for Christopher Newport, the resourceful seaman who brought the settlers to Jamestown in 1607 and made four more journeys between the Colony and the Virginia Company in London, a commuter and interpreter between two worlds.

He never knew what the Virginia Company's Council would want next. Once they ordered him to crown Powhatan. Nor did he ever know what he would find amiss in the Colony. Once he found the settlers preparing to hang John Smith.

But he had faith in the venture and persisted. So it's fitting that the city that launches ships bears his name.

But the sleepy little locality on a point of a 25-mile peninsula at the mouth of the James River awaited another adventurer.

Collis P. Huntington, 16-year-old traveling salesman from Connecticut, saw the prospect in 1837 when he was peddling watches and hardware for New England manufacturers. He remembered the site after the Civil War when he and his associates pushed the Central Pacific Railroad across the Sierra in 1869. Tall, with a great fan-beard and piercing eyes, Huntington looked the part of the empire builder.

He acquired control of the Chesapeake and Ohio Railway as a link in a transcontinental system. Looking for a port city terminus to handle coal from West Virginia mines, he selected Newport News. In 1885 he organized a dry dock and ship construction company, which got underway in 1889.

Under the impetus of World War I, its employe rolls increased to 7,500 in 1916, 9,500 in 1917, and finally to 12,500. In 18 months of war, it produced 25 destroyers and 12 other vessels.

The Disarmament Treaty of 1922 inaugurated a bleak era for the Shipyard. To hold the work force together, the Yard bid abnormally low to recondition the former German liner *Leviathan.* The job furnished work for almost 2,000 men for a year but ended in a loss of about $ 1.5 million. Shipyard President Homer T. Ferguson had a letter of resignation in his pocket when he went to inform Henry Huntington of the loss. Huntington, who had married his Uncle Collis' widow, told him, "My wife owns most of the stock in the Shipyard, and she has not been feeling too well recently, so maybe we should say no more about it."

In 1928 the shipyard received a contract for *Ranger 1,* the first ship to be designed as an aircraft carrier from the keel up. During World War II the Yard concentrated on carriers and delivered eight of the *Essex* class, one every 15 months. The total work force reached 31,000 employes, plus 21,000 at a subsidiary yard in Wilmington, N.C.

During the 1950s the Yard built the 990-foot passenger liner *United States,* and in 1961 built the first nuclear-powered aircraft carrier, the *Enterprise,* and followed with a virtual nuclear navy, including nuclear-powered Polaris-carrying submarines, nuclear attack submarines, and the newest nuclear-powered carriers, the *Dwight D. Eisenhower* and the *Nimitz.*

*Hampton Coliseum, the
first of the huge arenas
to pop up around Virginia,
like toadstools after
a spring rain, is seen at left
near Interstate 64.
By day, it looks like a white
coronet. At night
the fountain in the lagoon
blooms with changing lights,
and the series of tall
triangular panels around
the Coliseum blazes like the
setting for a ring. The
Coliseum is the showcase
for a variety of cultural
events and sports, including,
in the picture above,
ice hockey. When the circus
comes to Hampton Roads
Coliseum, motorists driving
by on Interstate 64 re-
duce speed at seeing a herd
of elephants lined
along the Coliseum's lagoon.*

Hampton's big Coliseum rises off Interstate

The *Nimitz,* named for Admiral Chester W. Nimitz who served as commander-in-chief of the U.S. Pacific Fleet during the war against Japan, is a swan-proud giant, weighing 95,000 tons, first of its class. It stretches 1,092 feet, is 252 feet wide at its extreme breadth, accomodates 6,286 persons and has a flight deck covering 4½ acres. It looks like a chunk of landscape, one of the mountainous wonders of Southwest Virginia displaced off course. But as fully compelling is the nuclear submarine.

She is not, at first glance, graceful.

Moored at pier, she looks as darkly somnolent and sullenly sluggish as a beached whale. She stretches longer than a football field, weighs more than a World War II light cruiser, and is shaped like a cigar, the plump variety that cartoonists used to put in the mouths of vested interests.

A mother of missiles, she is shaped, too, like the brood she berths, intercontinental ballistic missiles, lined upright inside her like waiting, unlit birthday candles, with more destructive force than all the bombs dropped in World War II.

She carries more electronic gear than nearly the entire submarine fleet of World War II. In event of an atomic war, she will make nearly any other kind of warship as obsolete as a canoe.

Her hull and superstructure are coated heavily with layers of preservative, anticorrosive paint, coal black, cold black, so as not to reflect the sun's rays, so as to absorb and extinguish any scintilla of light that filters to the oceans' depths. To stand on the tar-dark surface of her deck is to feel, briefly, you are on another, smaller planet, a dark asteroid.

Just forward of her superstructure's center rears a tall sail, like the center fin on a fish, housing six stack-like columns of detecting devices that can be raised silently to scan the sea and air.

A tug nurses her to sea, but, once underway on her own, she pushes back the hide of the ocean, and the faster she goes the more eagerly her nose dips, as if, in her teardrop design, she wishes to mingle, get lost, with the surrounding waters. Awkward on the surface, she is as free as a whale beneath it. (Sometimes, say the sailors, she has come up near whales, rolling and blowing, and they paid her no more heed than one of their own.)

Her 30-foot deep interior has three decks, with every square inch tightly blueprinted for use, batteries of buttons, moving marquees of lights. Two crews man her. When one team has her at sea, the other platoon is ashore on leave and on training. The men have a lounge, stereo recorders in their bunks, movies in the mess, exercise machines, a library. But when she descends into her silent world, she can only receive, not send, messages. Her crew members cannot indulge in the serviceman's solace, writing letters home, but their families are permitted a few familygrams a month, composed with the care of a poet writing a sonnet: Sally got all A's . . . She can travel a hundred thousand miles without surfacing. No place is out of reach of her missile. Covering a target a thousand miles inland, she would have 8.2 million square miles in which to hide, a dark straw in a black haystack.

A missile can be fired only by a team effort, hedged with a series of safeguards. But what about the checks and balances in the minds of the crew? How does it feel to tend constantly a weapon one prays never will be fired in hostility? The sailors' answer is that the sub is a safeguard, a deterrent. They are, they believe, the peace-keepers.

In 1968 Tenneco purchased the Yard as a subsidiary. In 1972 it began constructing the largest drydock in the Western hemisphere. Measuring 1,600 feet long, 230 feet wide, and 44 feet deep, it enables Newport News to build supercarriers and liquified natural gas carriers.

Close by the Yard is the Mariners Museum where the nautical minded can immerse themselves in the seas' curios. The museum was endowed by Archer M. Huntington, son of Collis Huntington. It is surrounded by 800 acres, much of it in a natural state, other parts filled with statuary, including the work of the founder's wife, Anna Hyatt Huntington, a little woman with an imagination that produced such large figures as a life-sized mountain lion.

A mammoth golden eagle, a ship figurehead with a wingspread of more than 18 feet, weighing 3,200 pounds, greets the visitor in the main gallery. In the museum are 85 other figureheads. Mounted on the wall and tilted forward as on the bows of ships, they stare blindly ahead.

Over all in the main gallery flashes beams of light, whirling specks of gold from the prism of a large revolving lighthouse lens. The Mariners Museum came near being psychedelic before the flower children did. One may see the gondola said to have been used by Robert and Elizabeth Barrett Browning on their honeymoon, two whale boats fully equipped, ready for Ahab, and Mark Twain's pilot license for the Mississippi.

So what of Hampton, Newport News's big sister?

She is quite a lady.

The oldest continuous English settlement (1610) in America, Hampton has at NASA's Langley Research Center the cradle of the space age.

And the cradle is still rocking, still producing research to back America's space flights.

Here the astronauts learned to walk.

Hampton is to air and outer space what Newport News is to water.

Langley Air Force Base, the Nation's oldest active military air installation, is headquarters for the Tactical Air Command, as it has been for more than a quarter of a century.

(The Army also has its boots planted solidly in Hampton, with Fort Monroe, whose 1819 moat surrounds the oldest fort in continuous use.)

Langley Research Center, the senior field establishment of the National Aeronautics and Space

At the Mariners Museum in Newport News, the nautical minded may immerse their minds in the seas' curios. In the main gallery, they confront an eagle figurehead with an 18-foot wingspread, the gondola the Brownings used on their honeymoon, and whaleboats ready for Captain Ahab.
At left, tanks line the way to the Virginia War Memorial Museum, which has relics from eight wars, including Artillery Capt. Harry Truman's brass hat.

Golden eagle greets visitors to museum

Langley Center houses research for Nation's space program

Five huge vacuum spheres gleam like silver cocoons from which come solutions to space problems. At the Langley Research Center the astronauts learned to walk on the moon and to maneuver their landing craft. Here, too, scientists plan and test manned space laboratories, and crape myrtle bloom.

Nuclear-powered aircraft carrier Nimitz, the first in her class, awaits finishing touches in Newport News. Named for A

z, the carrier weighs 95,000 tons, stretches 1,092ft., accommodates 6,286 persons, and has a flight deck of 4,5 acres.

Newport News
Yard is State's
largest private
source of jobs

Newport News Shipbuilding and Dry Dock Company builds a nuclear navy from submarines to carriers. In picture above are pens for constructing nuclear subs. At right, statue of empire builder Collis P. Huntington, who founded the shipyard in 1885, gestures towards "the earth's best half acre," his yard. Below, left, idle shipyard workers lounge downtown Newport News. Yard hives 18,000 for big jobs.

Administration, was founded long before NASA. President Woodrow Wilson ordered it in 1917. Until 1940, it was the only national laboratory for aeronautical research.

Named in honor of pioneering scientist Samuel Pierpont Langley, the Research Center has pioneered consistently.

Research already underway at Langley made it possible for NASA to launch plans for manned space flight in Project Mercury, only a few days after NASA had been founded in 1958. Personnel from Langley formed the Space Task Force which managed the Mercury program and later established the NASA Manned Space Craft Center at Houston, Texas.

The first seven astronauts, Alan Shepard and his brethren, learned to walk and run in the moon's gravitational field, dressed in a space suit, harnessed in slings, cables, and trolley of a simulator, like a child suited up for a cold day in a walker.

They and their successors practiced landing on the moon in Langley's Lunar Landing Research Facility, a gleaming silver and red structure reared against the blue sky as if built from a boy's erector set, a steel gantry 250 feet high and 400 feet long. A manned rocket-powered research vehicle, a four-legged, disk-footed contraption, dropped on a line from the top of the erector set like a creature out of Dr. Seuss.

Prominent on Langley's skyline are five huge vacuum spheres, like puff balls on a forest floor, or silver cocoons out of which were spun solutions to problems posed by high-speed flights. Seven Hampton bridges over small creeks bear the names of the original astronauts. There are enough creeks threading Hampton to furnish names for space heroes for the next half century.

An effect of Langley and other Federal installations has been to infuse ideas and talent into the governments of Hampton and Newport News, especially their school systems.

Hampton already had the oldest continuous free schools and the first endowed educational institution in the United States. (Continuous is an adjective applied continually to Hampton.) In 1634 Benjamin Syms left 200 acres and 8 cows in his will for a free school for the children of the parish. In 1659 Thomas Eaton, 'cururgeon,' left 500 acres and everything on it for a school to serve old Elizabeth City County. In 1805 they were merged into Hampton Academy and in 1852 became part of the public school system.

Not content with having their children in the oldest schools space-age personnel wish to have them enrolled among some of the best.

Another historic and innovative educational facility is Hampton Institute, founded by the American Missionary Association at the instigation of General Samuel Chapman Armstrong, chief of the Freedmen's Bureau. The school sprang out of a desire of freed men, women, and children to learn

to read after the Emancipation Proclamation. The gathered under the trees to call their ABCs. Th school opened in 1868 with Armstrong as principa

Langley's impact on Hampton's intellectual en vironment was felt clearly with the election of Mr Ann Kilgore as Mayor in 1959. Wife of the depu chief of the Research Center's engineering an technical services, Mrs. Kilgore gave the City a exciting administration, from the creation of 5 public kindergartens to the building of Hampto Coliseum. (Her successor as Mayor, David Mor tague, somewhat a rarity himself in being a Re publican, continued the pace.) Businessman Tho mas Chisman spurred downtown redevelopment.

Hampton's assertive spirit was symbolized in it becoming the first Virginia city to construct coliseum. When Hampton and Newport Ne couldn't agree on a site, Mrs. Kilgore inspired he city to push ahead.

The Hampton Coliseum sits off Interstate 64, creamy metaphor of a building, its hinged, high pointed panels like so many sails or kites. It look to be a coronet, the tart ate by the Jack of Heart and, at night when the panels are flooded in ligh a brilliant setting of diamonds in a ring. When th circus comes to town, the elephants amble betwee shows onto a peninsula extending into the Col seum's lagoon. Passing motorists on the intersta reduce speed at the sight of the huge structure an the nodding gray beasts that, for once, are in sca with their surroundings. Nothing inside can top th free show out in the open. The Hampton Coliseu is hard to beat as a setting for elephants at eas

Newport News and Hampton sit at the head Hampton Roads. Writing in 1868 in the Nor American Review about the potential of th magnificent harbor, Charles Francis Adams note that if nature ever heaped upon any place its blessir it was at Norfolk, but there nature had not bee seconded by man.

Not only had man not seconded nature f Hampton Roads. Writing in 1868 in the Nor mid-1800s Virginia's cities at the fall line checke any effort to enhance the ocean ports.

In the mid-1950s, with the creation of the Vi ginia State Ports Authority, the General Assemb recognized that the ports of Newport News, No folk, and Portsmouth offered a natural resour that should be developed for the Commonwealth benefit. But the Authority proved, for the mos only advisory, and the competitive instincts of th three cities was too strong for them voluntarily pull together for long in the same boat. Governo Godwin appointed a commission to study uni cation of three ports under State direction, and 1972, coaxed by Governor Holton, the three citi united their port facilities under the Virginia Po Authority. Increasing toll-free crossings of Ham ton Roads offered other assurance that the citi by the sea, brought together, could work as one.

Cities by the sea

Norfolk is on the move, its admirers say.

A visitor drives west on Waterfront Drive toward the center of the city, and when the clean-cut, monolithic structures of the revived downtown swim into view, it looks, as the car sweeps along the expressway's guard rail, as if, indeed, the buildings are physically moving before the motorist's eyes, that they are shifting about at the urging of a giant, unseen hand in some game of chess with destiny.

Norfolk, quite plainly, is moving.

Nobody's born in Norfolk, they also say.

And truly such installations as the headquarters for the North Atlantic Treaty Organization, and the Armed Forces Staff College, plus the Norfolk Naval Base and the ports, contribute to a polyglot population.

(Norfolk is reputed to have fewer spinsters than any other city in the Nation. The world's largest naval base supplies a variety of escort vessels from the newest bluejackets to retired admirals.)

Of course, Norfolk has a sizeable stock of natives, the base, indeed, of its alphabet soup of states and nationalities.

But in any gathering newcomers usually outnumber Norfolk-born. There is a heavy strain of Eastern North Carolinians who from the beginning have looked more to Norfolk than Raleigh. Norfolk sometimes is called the Capital of Eastern North Carolina.

And Norfolk, at odds with the rest of Virginia in its early history, swore that when the going got rough it just might leave the Old Dominion for the Old North State.

In 1849, after the state blocked the city from access to canals and railroads, a reader wrote the *Norfolk Argus* that he was "for hitching teams with the Old North State for it has long been my notion that Virginia cares little for Norfolk. We cannot be worse off and we may be better. Huzza for North Carolina and annexation!"

For years, nearly as long as South and North Carolina and Virginia have existed, North Carolina has been described as "a valley of humility between two mountains of conceit."

A noted second-generation immigrant in Norfolk prefers to characterize North Carolina as "the Scotland of Virginia."

Meaning that the Tarheels who come across the border are gripped primarily with the notion of getting ahead, not looking back, and bring vitality.

The alliance between Norfolk and North Carolina goes back two centuries when Tarheel farmers and fishermen brought harvests overland or around the coast to market and then through a canal cut from Norfolk to the great North Carolina Sounds.

Norfolk's difference with the rest of Virginia traces to the city's roots.

In 1680 Charles II became dissatisfied with the way his Old Dominion was developing. Why are there no towns? His Majesty demanded.

There was no role for them. English ships sailed up the rivers and creeks that veined Virginia and stopped at every plantation wharf to unload goods from London and take on cured tobacco. Nevertheless the King was uneasy. He was used to citizens being clustered where he and his tax collectors could lay hands on them easily.

At the King's command to bring forth towns, the Assembly required each county to set aside 50 acres, and the Lower Norfolk County Court selected a site at the entrance to the Eastern Branch of the Elizabeth River. The King vetoed the act in 1681, too late. Norfolk was on the way.

The passage was to prove tumultuous.

Anything dire that happened to Virginia seemed bound to hit Norfolk the hardest.

It was the city of adversity.

Nor did the planters seen to mind what happened to the town in their agricultural Eden.

Norfolk, a city
of adversity,
has brave face

Looking west, a motorist gazes past guardrails at Norfolk's bold skyline of civic center, banks, and church spires, urban renewal's doing. It seems that the buildings are moving before his eyes.

The other cities by the sea are Virginia Beach, Virginia's ample sandpile, Portsmouth and its Naval Hospital and shipyard named for Norfolk, and fast-growing Chesapeake with Dismal Swamp.

Old St. Paul's has a shot in its wall from Dunmore

Among old churches that bless Tidewater are a pair of saints: St. Paul's in Norfolk built in 1739, bombarded in 1776 by the British, and squat St. Luke's built only the Lord knows when in Smithfield. There the faithful flock yearly to pray.

FIRED BY
LORD DUNMORE
JAN. 1, 1776.

Norfolk was the come-back kid.

On its own.

Every step forward seemed to be followed by two or more backward.

First there came an advance. English ships, increasing in size and finding it difficult to navigate creeks and rivers, made Norfolk their wharf for all Tidewater.

Visiting Norfolk in 1728, William Byrd II wrote, "The two cardinal virtues that make a place thrive, industry and frugality, are seen here in perfection."

Norfolk's population had swelled to 6,000 by 1776. But that year, on January 1, Lord Dunmore's warships bombarded the town, and British sailors came ashore and set fire to warehouses, whereupon American soldiers, who felt they couldn't hold the place, also put the torch to it. Abandoning the town in February, the Colonials set fire to the remaining 400 or so dwellings. Norfolk burned down.

Norfolk was the only city in the new Nation to be burned by both sides.

One brick structure that escaped, and still stands, was St. Paul's Church. Set in a grove of trees, surrounded now by urban renewal, Old St. Paul's has a British cannonball lodged in its east wall, a shot in Norfolk's craw typifying the city's gritty destiny.

The ball, after striking St. Paul's, dropped to the ground, but the citizens mortised it into the dent. So popular a landmark is the shot that a sign stuck in the ground directs the curious TO THE CANNONBALL. Twelve inches to the right, and it would have missed the corner of the church – and a place in the Norfolk Tour. But that – making the most of what few heirlooms it has – is part of the Norfolk way.

After the war when English and Scottish merchants came over to set up shop, Portsmouth turned them away, but Norfolk, devastated, opened its arms to any source that wished to invest in its future.

(In 1963 former City Manager C. A. Harrell, who had helped shape Norfolk's resurgence after World War II, returned for a civic banquet and observed that the city early learned a lesson: to be part of an experiment advancing mankind is enobling but there are two kinds of guinea pigs – the ones that die and those that survive, and Norfolk early found it better to be among the latter.)

Outbreak of war in Europe in 1792 boosted American shipping and Norfolk's recovery – but under Jefferson's Embargo of 1807 and the British blockade in the War of 1812, Norfolk relapsed.

No other American city suffered as much as Norfolk in the Nation's first two wars.

Hampton Roads offers scenes that change every second

Below, men and boys and fish in the shallows of Roads where ironclads Monitor and Merrimac fought during the Civil War for supremacy of sea, thundering, bouncing shells off each other's sides. It was a draw. But naval war was never the same. The men and boys probably are fishing for spot, unexcelled for flavor.

Middle Ground Light is
red-clad traffic cop
in the middle of the Roads
past which crawl
tankers so long the skipper
uses TV to see the
bow. In Norfolk's office
towers workers watch
craft skim away, and wish
they could. A confeder-
ate atop a 50-foot pedestal,
Johnny Reb, guards
Norfolk's bank buildings.

Norfolk's scope blazes in the night, a beacon for culture in an urban renewal area that was once choked with slums.

hrysler Hall. Behind it is the City Hall, its roof rimmed in light. The financial district fills the skyline with lights.

Hampton Roads harbors liner United States, jet aircraft

A pleasure boat speeds by the United States, the fastest, longest, largest liner we ever built. Her forward stack soars 175 feet, 17 stories. She weighs 52,000 tons, extends 990 feet, has 12 decks and quarters for 2,000 plus crew, and holds the Blue Riband for fastest crossing of the Atlantic both ways. She cost $72 million to build in Newport News, and now the luxury liner rests in Norfolk International Terminal, retired. Oceana Naval Air Station shelters 20 squadrons, with seven miles of runways from which they fly.

212

Guided missile frigate Farragut rests at Norfolk Naval Operating Station, while a busy, blunt-nosed harbor tug goes about its chores. The giant naval base, established in 1917, has responded swiftly and surely to the demands of all the Nation's wars and crises.

Sightseers on the harbor tour pass vintage warships close by the Norfolk Naval Shipyard. Hampton Roads is the channel through which the James, Nansemond, and Elizabeth Rivers flow to the Bay.

Norfolk, Naval Capital of the United States, holds place on Hampton Roads

215

216

Nothing offers
faster relief
from heat than
plunging
through surf at
Virginia Beach

*No one has to buy a ticket
join a club, register
in a motel, rent a cabana
to enjoy the beach.
Every foot of 38 miles
is open to anyone.
All a body need do is walk
onto the sand, or,
if he'd rather, then stretch
on the warm sand
and doze in the hot sun,
waken now and then,
run groggily to the ocean,
fall in its cold
depths, come up gasping,
shocked, then march
back up the beach to sleep
or studiously watch
a wave forming down the*

*way and try to figure
the exact spot it
will hit the beach. Listen
to old Wordsworth
and see the children sport
upon the shore
and hear the mighty waters
rolling evermore.*

Annual
Boardwalk
Art Show
runs five days
in mid-July

*Who would object to going
to an exhibition
where the 10-block gallery
is a boardwalk,
the backdrop is the whole
Atlantic Ocean,
the artists are the models,
and the blazing sun
is the master painter that
lightens the scene?
Which is droller, the squat,
gnome-like creature
or the spectators gathered
curiously in much
its same stance to view it?
They shake their
heads in wonder and ask
"Is THAT art?"*

218

219

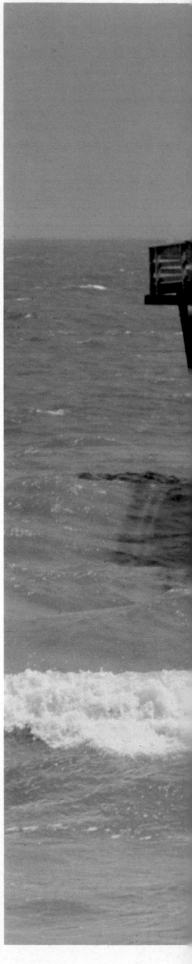

Tell us, how is the fishing on the pier?

Fishermen congregate on the pier as thickly as hungry gulls on a sandspit. To the fish it makes little difference whether it is caught from the spit or from the crowded pier.

Virginia Beach provides haven for birds

200,000 guests come to dinner in October in National Back Bay Wildlife Refuge. Geese ducks, swans flock from the north to make the marshes their winter home. The refuge, founded in 1938, has 9,000 acres. Back Bay

s one of the smallest
ut also one of the most im-
ortant refuges on the
East Coast flyway.
In the photographs at left
a flock of cattle
egrets, African immigrants,
white cloud,
while American egrets keep
watch in trees.

There's refuge for man in
Seashore State Park's
2,700 wilderness acres
where knobby-kneed
cypress trees drapping gray
Spanish moss stand
in black-stained water. The
blazing noon sun
barely filters through the
canopy of leaves.

Norfolk was reviving when it received another setback in the 1830s. Faced with encouraging railroads or canals, the General Assembly took the wrong risk by investing $ 100,000 in the James River and Kanawha Company to build a canal between Richmond and Lynchburg. Further, the Piedmont interests saw to it that railroads terminated at the fall-line towns instead of extending to the seaport.

In 1833 when Norfolk tried to connect a rail line with Roanoke, Petersburg's backers killed a request for aid in the State Senate. The *Norfolk Herald* responded: "Well, go on gentlemen, you have for a time succeeded…but you have not put us down. With our own resources we will complete the railway."

There spoke the Little Red Hen of Virginia's cities.

But, handicapped by the state's faulty gamble on canals and by the rivalry between Piedmont and Tidewater, neither Norfolk nor the other Virginia towns moved as early or rapidly as Baltimore, which extended the Baltimore and Ohio into the western market.

The penalty for Virginia's ineffectual policy for internal improvements, wrote Thomas J. Wertenbaker, was "swift and terrible. In the Civil War Virginia needed warships to break the blockade and protect her commerce, but the discrimination against her one natural port made the creation of a navy most difficult; she needed the support of all sections of the state, but the isolation of the western counties left them no alternative save separation; she needed a network of modern railways to move and supply her own troops, but her mileage was comparatively low, her lines improperly located; she needed all her sons to fight her battles, but tens of thousands of young Virginians had gone west to seek new opportunities and build new homes."

Dr. Wertenbaker's work, updated in 1962 by Marvin W. Schlegel – *Norfolk, Historic Southern Port* – is a model local history, evidence of Norfolk's determination to go first-class, even to the telling of her past.

But against the view that Virginia's lack of rail lines handicapped the Confederacy may be weighed the possibility that had the great port been developed at a pace with Baltimore and New York and had rail lines connected Virginia with the Midwest and the East, then, tied closely to the prosperous, bustling Union, the Commonwealth might never have seceded.

Sometimes it seemed that Norfolk dwelled with the Four Horsemen of the Apocalypse.

In 1795, 1802, 1821, 1826, and in 1855 yellow fever afflicted the city. In 1855 only the coming of frost broke the pestilence that took nearly 2,000 lives. From that ordeal Norfolk plunged into the Civil War. For three years the city suffered occupation, most of the time under General Benjamin "Beast" Butler, who closed schools, seized funds that had been set aside for children orphaned by the plague, and arrested and insulted paroled Confederates. He simply had a genius for being beastly.

An elderly Norfolkian, a veteran of civic drives, pondered the disasters from the cannonball on, and, sighing as if he had experienced every one of them, said, "It's just been one thing after another, hasn't it?"

No community better deserves to be represented by the phoenix rising from the ashes. Yet so disposed are the Norfolkians generally to look ahead, without much reflection on what has gone before, that the leadership in every era is under the illusion that it sparked the city's rejuvenation.

After the Civil War prosperity came to Norfolk along with a half dozen railroad lines. Then Norfolk outbid Richmond for the Jamestown Tercentennial Exhibition of 1907, which caught the Nation's attention – although, as might have been expected, various setbacks, including the weather, prevented the show from getting into full swing until September, when it was almost over. With the outbreak of World War I the Navy settled on Norfolk as the site for the world's largest Naval Base. The Navy and Norfolk formed a steadily deepening alliance, and Norfolk came to look on the Federal Government as a partner, not an opponent. When other cities hung back from requesting Federal aid, Norfolk turned eagerly to Washington.

It became the Nation's "Capital of the Navy," headquarters for the Atlantic fleet and for NATO, site of the Norfolk Naval Base, and, to boot, the Little Creek Amphibious Base, training station for fleet Marines in the Atlantic, and, further, the Dam Neck training center for personnel in nuclear missile submarines.

Federal grants and payrolls bolster Hampton Roads' economy, and the military population contributes to the area's elan. Service personnel have a sensitivity to their surroundings characteristic of individuals who know that at a moment's notice they may be plucked out of it and planted somewhere else. Husbands, wives, and children have the air of being able to function gracefully in any situation, because, really, the new to them is the status quo. The children fit easily into one school after another. Wives find jobs – the local school systems especially are enriched by their presence – form friendships, and soon are entertaining as if they have been born in the community.

Listening to career officers chatting about a shop they know near Tokyo that sells silk screens or a tailor to be recommended in Hong Kong or a restaurant not to be missed in Frankfurt, the ordinary Virginian suddenly is aware of a life as foreign to him as a gypsy's existence. That service families thrive on it is shown by the frequency

The ship on the horizon is different, but the land is not much changed from the way the colonists saw it when they stopped on the way to Jamestown, planted a cross, and opened the Virginia Company's box of instructions.

with which three or four generations on both sides are at home in the military.

Not only do they take part in civic causes while stationed in Hampton Roads but many retire there, and the younger ones, in their late 40s and early 50s, make it the scene of their second career. Hampton Roads is, next to San Diego, the military's second most popular area in the United States for retirement. And it is gaining on San Diego, thanks to the resurgence that began in Norfolk and spread throughout Hampton Roads following World War II.

During Norfolk Mayor Pretlow Darden's reform administration, City Council risked $ 25,000 on a study that would prepare the city for Federal housing funds, should any become available. They did, and in 1949 Norfolk became the first city to execute a loan and grant under the new law.

The Norfolk urban renewal program ripped out some of the worst slums in the United States. The devastation was such that some wondered if Norfolk would ever put itself together again. Norfolk, newcomers observe, is always digging up dirt and throwing it around.

The city's readiness for Federal aid extended to other opportunities. Mayor Fred Duckworth's administration converted the old City Hall into a mausoleum and museum for General Douglas MacArthur. (The army Captain lies in the Naval Capital because his mother was born there.) When Mayor Roy Martin's administration heard that Walter P. Chrysler Jr. was looking for a place to deposit his multimillion dollar art collection, Norfolk opened it's art museum to him. With two-thirds Federal aid, the city built Scope, a cultural and convention center, a lovely curve on the city's skyline, half a sphere exposed, as if the arc extended on under the earth to complete the circle. Approaching Scope, the visitor sees the patch of a floating dome with something of the excitement that used to attend the first glimpse of a weather-bleached circus tent shining in the sun.

Economic competition between Richmond and Norfolk dwindled in the 20th century to spasmodic, good-natured boasting about which was the largest city, and by the 1960s each was so beset with problems of a core city that it was not disposed to do much guying of the other. They were companions in misery.

Their styles are in rich contrast: Richmond, a cohesive city, solid, secure, steadily growing around a downtown as firmly fixed as a sun, so that even its name – Rich-mond – sounds like a declaration of confidence; Norfolk, slung out, sprawling, fragmented by rivers and creeks, an exploding nova that might coalesce some day or might continue flying apart, so even its most active leaders trying to sum it up, intone the name with a question in their voices – Naw-folk? – as if it were one thing today and might be something entirely different tomorrow. You scarcely can pronounce Norfolk without sounding argumentative. Once a General Assembly member approached Norfolk Senator Stanley Walker to inquire if he thought Norfolk would consider a certain controversial measure. Consider it? said Mr. Walker. Norfolk will con-sider anything!

Residents of each city sometimes have exaggerated notions about the other. Richmonders, having heard of Norfolk's so-called radical tendencies, are taken aback when they visit the clean, serene, modernistic civic center on the waterfront. Norfolkians, having scoffed at Richmond's supposed stand-pat attitudes, often, once they stay a while, fall under its spell, and leave, if at all, unwillingly.

A Norfolk native, E. Griffith Dodson, Clerk of the House of Delegates for 28 years, divided his time between the two cities and loved both. When he arrived in Richmond to assume the duties of Clerk, someone asked how he liked Richmond.

"I would rather live in Richmond than go to heaven!" boomed Colonel Dodson. Then, while the company was digesting that affirmation, he added, "If I went to heaven, I couldn't go to Norfolk."

Richmond is stone, well-based, granite gray monuments and State office buildings, the stable seat of government, the Rome of Virginia. Norfolk is water, fluid, often roiled, changing currents and colors.

Much-tested Norfolk became the target of the State's school-closing Massive Resistance laws that shut down six high schools for five months in 1958–59. It rallied, and, although sorely tried, became a pace-setter for the South in school desegregation.

Across the Elizabeth River from vaulting Norfolk is Portsmouth. It feels toward Norfolk some of the competitiveness that Norfolk feels toward the rest of Virginia. Portsmouth is in the challenging position of being No. 2 to a No. 2 that always is trying harder. Yet the two cities are, or ought to be, one. A glance at an urban renewal map shows that the blighted area lies in a scythe across their downtowns, interrupted only briefly by the river. Their problems are mutual, whether or not they unite in solving them.

Sometimes it seems to Portsmouth that everything falls Norfolk's way. Portsmouth has even had to resign itself to hearing its great shipbuilding yard being called the Norfolk Naval Shipyard.

The oldest in the United States, the Yard began when Andrew Sprowle, a Scot, built a marine yard and tenemients and started the village of Gosport, named after the town opposite Portsmouth, England. In November 1767 the British Government took over the yard as a repair station and appointed Sprowle navy agent. With Governor James Monroe's assent in 1801, the Federal Government purchased the yard – and made its first sizeable in-

The living and fishing is easy in places such as these

The scene could be Dismal Swamp or a number of choice backwaters, but it happens to be the Chickahominy Swamp. No doubt the trio is hoping that a largemouth bass will bite. Lunker-sized bass from 7 to 11 pounds can be found in most of the Commonwealth's rivers, lakes, and ponds. The largemouth must be classed as a most democratic fish.

vestment in Tidewater. It now is the largest shipyard in the world for repair and conversion.

The Portsmouth Naval Hospital, which opened in 1830, is the Nation's oldest — and one of its most modern — naval hospitals. Within a few blocks of the downtown Civic Center is Olde Town, a 12-block square of homes dating back to the Revolution and beyond, and shaded in many instances by trees nearly as old.

Portsmouth is next door to Suffolk, the world's greatest purveyor of peanuts, raw, roasted, chocolate-covered. Suffolk shares with the neighboring City of Chesapeake Virginia's 43,200 acres of the Dismal Swamp. Once large as Rhode Island, two-thirds of Dismal laps over into five North Carolina counties.

William Byrd II helped survey the swamp — and pronounced it dismal. George Washington formed with five others a company for draining it, and various entrepreneurs have been cutting and plowing it ever since.

There's no more contrary piece of real estate in Virginia than Old Dismal. Instead of being a low place into which streams drain, it is higher than the surrounding country, a well-saturated peat-sponge that feeds a dozen rivers and Lake Drummond. The three-mile long lake is an amber jewel named for North Carolina's first Governor, William Drummond. He sided with Nathaniel Bacon and was hanged at Governor Berkeley's order.

Virginians find comfort in the thought that Old Dismal is there, plunked down in the middle of a vast, growing metropolis. In 1973 Union Camp Corporation donated 50,000 acres as a preserve.

Beyond Suffolk is Smithfield. It is nearly impossible to get through Smithfield without stopping. First off, there is the Smithfield ham, most famous of Virginia's viands. Royal Governors used to send it back to England. Any land that produced such a delicacy could not be dismissed as uncivilized.

The heavenly haunch originated when the Jamestown settlers herded their hogs for safekeeping onto an island in the James — it's still called Hog Island — where the animals fattened on nuts, herbs, and roots, a diet that gave the meat an oily quality.

Only an oily specimen can hold up under the curing, drying, and ripening period of at least nine months. The settlers refined the process from the Indians' practice of smoking venison over fires of oak, applewood, and hickory.

Selected carefully, rubbed with salt and cooled a month or so, washed and peppered and then smoked for a week, hung from rafters to mellow for a year or more, the Smithfield ham, like a Rembrandt, can't be hurried.

Indeed, the 1922 General Assembly fixed it in law as a ham cut from the carcass of a peanut-fed hog raised in the peanut belt of Virginia or North Carolina and treated, smoked, or processed in Smithfield. The 1968 General Assembly removed

227

the qualification that the hog be peanut-fed because soy beans had proved just as efficacious. But there's been no fudging with the rest of the process.

As might be expected, a ham that takes so long in curing requires care in cooking, too. The chef must soak the ham overnight, boil it, skin it, sprinkle it with brown sugar, dot it with cloves, bake it, and then eat it. Oh – and slice it thin, for any ham so prepared has been reduced to the very essence of its goodness. Even a smidgin goes a long way.

Smithfield's other point of interest is the Old Brick Church, or St. Luke's, built in 1632, its sturdy tower giving it the look of a fort, and purposely so, perhaps, as offering worshippers protection against an Indian attack. The bricks, laid in Flemish bond, were cemented with mortar made of oyster-shell lime.

Every May there's a homecoming, or pilgrimage, with a sermon, followed by a dinner on the grounds prepared by the women of the church and featuring Smithfield ham, a day nourishing body and soul.

Driving Route 10 into Smithfield from Norfolk the traveler dips down and crosses a bridge over the Pagan River and immediately his eye is filled with marshes. He rides into town, and every gap between stores or houses offers a glimpse of marshland below: yellow, brown, or green, depending on the season. They don't need calendars in Smithfield; all they do is look at the marshes and know that they are experiencing an April chartreuse or an October beige.

Virginia Beach is rightly named. For it is, indeed, the Beach for all Virginia. In the 1972 General Assembly's closing hours the members had agreed not to permit any amendments to the State Budget – but they opened it to a request for funds to replenish sand on Virginia Beach, because the beach, they reasoned, belonged to everybody.

Every foot of Virginia Beach's 38 miles of shoreline has a reward for the senses, the basic delight, perhaps, being the freedom to walk without hindrance along the sand in sight and sound of the surf. No one has to pay a fee, join a club, rent a cabana, or register in a motel to savor Virginia Beach. You simply walk onto it.

And if you are too tired to walk, then flop on the sand and watch the tumbling hills of glistening salt-white surf and study the curving blade of a wave running gleaming along the shore. Or if that is too demanding, simply close the eyes and listen to the waves, first the general roar, and then, bit by bit, individual sounds coming through: a tearing noise, as if a canvas sky is splitting apart, a loud thunderclap, like a shot, as a wave slaps the sand, and sometimes – and this is what you listen for most intently – just before the next tumbling roar, a split second of absolute silence, as if the whole vast heaving ocean had paused to listen to itself.

For five days in mid-July the annual Boardwalk Art Show spreads paintings, prints, drawings, ceramics, and sculpture 10 blocks along the shore. It is a toss-up as to which is the more diverting, the art or the people looking at it. The dazzling sun sweeps the scene like a paint brush, heightening the colors, highlighting the shapes. Surely it is the world's most pleasant gallery, the Atlantic Ocean its backdrop. And if artist or spectator tires of the panorama, he or she can run to the shore, plunge under the tingling surf, and wash away frustrations.

Piers in the water off Virginia Beach and Norfolk's Ocean View Beach are as thronged with people fishing as is a sand spit with gulls. Like as not, if it's early fall, they are fishing for spot. It is the smallest of the saltwater fish – no larger than a woman's hand from tip of the little finger to wrist – and also among the tastiest and most plentiful. When spot are running, fishermen return laden with catches of 40 or 50 or more.

The spot isn't overpowering in size or flavor. Rolled in corn meal and fried, first with the lid on the pan for cooking through and through and then with it off for browning, and served hot and crisp with batter bread, corn cakes, or hoecake, the spot is a breakfast that stays with a person through the day, and, in wistful recollection, the weeks.

With someone who doesn't care for fish, you had best start him on spot, and gently. Show how easily the meat is reached – turn back the crust, lift out the bone, and there the bounty is – let him sniff the fragrance, and – but don't prod him – nibble a bit and catch the flavor that, while distinctive, is light and delicate, and he is hooked. If the Lord passed out spot on the shore of Galilee, then the multitude was well-fed.

Virginia Beach bills itself as a Resort City, but it is much more – a mixture of farms, shopping centers, and bedroom communities to Norfolk.

In 1963 Princess Anne County merged with the Borough of Virginia Beach to produce a city with 77 per cent of its land still undeveloped and 40 per cent of it still being farmed.

Residents of Pungo still think of themselves as living "down in the country." And in country stores one occasionally picks up stories of the sort that used to flourish and are now becoming rare as passenger pigeons.

About the new clerk, for instance, who was approached by an old-timer who asked for a half a length of stove pipe, as customers used to do in the Depression. The puzzled clerk excused himself and walked in the back of the store to consult the owner. "Some damn fool out there wants to buy a half a length of stove pipe," the clerk was saying, and, turning and seeing that the customer had followed him, he added, hastily, "and this nice gentleman wants to buy the other half!"

2 lighthouses dominate sky at Cape Henry

Black-and-white tower guides ships into the Bay. Old gray ghost, built in 1791, is a lookout for tourists who can see at a glance Virginia Beach, Seashore State Park, and the point where the colonists landed.

Anyway, amid the streaming traffic of Virginia Beach, one of the Commonwealth's fastest growing cities, you come upon broad fields blinking sleepily in the sun, and in certain seasons can, if you like, get out of the car and pick strawberries and pull your own corn, for a fraction of what they cost in the super markets.

For those in a hurry there are road-side markets, ranging in scope from a lean-to to a line of many stalls. Truly, it is a heart- (or stomach-) satisfying spectacle: the green ranks of corn along the way, tall, tasseled, thick-massed as Caesar's legions waiting the order to march, to the fray, or the table; the jumble of watermelons by a stand, as if somebody had collected the great guffaws at a good joke and piled them there, mirth made visible; heaping bushel baskets of tomatoes set under a great oak, some flaring fire-bright in the sun, others quietly red in the shade, a checkered expanse, and trays of the more exotic vegetables – furry okra and jade-green peppers, sullen purple eggplant, clustered pearl-white spring onions, wrenched from the ground, and beets that bleed when cut, all of the provender dirt-fresh.

Virginia Beach, always wanting something else, should take stock and cherish what it has: an unrivaled shore and backing it up, an overflowing cornucopia of good things to eat. Instead of fiddling with illusions of electronic industries and oil refineries, zone the land for light and heavy vegetables, especially if planners are to be believed in their predictions of a zillion people 20 years hence. (People will accept any projection if you make it big enough and so far ahead that there is nothing they have to do about it right now.) The Chamber of Commerce might supply motel rooms with maps directing famished tourists to the farms, and the Governor order a freeze to keep families where they have been working miracles.

Virginia Beach is an important stop on two major flyways. Naval Air Station Oceana, a complex of more than seven miles of runways, serves the East Coast's military air traffic, one of two master jet bases in the Eastern United States, home of 20 fighter and attack squadrons flying the Navy's most advanced aircraft.

On November 25, 1940 the United States Government purchased 328 acres for a small airfield. Immediately after the Japanese attacked Pearl Harbor, the base began expanding. As Oceana entered the 1970s it was a community of 22,000 people on more than 8,000 acres of land.

Vacationers sunning on the beach look up and mark the vapor trail of a jet piercing the blue like an ice pick traveling through a block of ice.

But on the other hand, walking the beach in October, they raise their eyes at the sound of a honking and see the long-necked silhouettes of Canada geese.

For a mile or so down the beach is the National Back Bay Wildlife Refuge which welcomes 200,000 guests every October, an assortment of widgeon, greater snow geese, whistling swans, Canada geese, black ducks and mallards, and other fowl.

When the population is clamoring and gabbling in the marsh, taking off and landing in swirling clouds of feathers, "it puts you in another world," says Romie Waterfield, a 20-year employe, who was reared in nearby Wash Woods. (There's a Waterfield, or someone like him, in every wilderness area, a student of all that's going on.)

He has seen the marsh's broad reaches completely white with snow geese.

"You just forget everything else," he said.

On the other hand, "the plainest bird you find here, if you really look at him, is beautiful. Even the old American bittern, if you look closely, is a handsome fellow, with his greenish yellow eyes and his habit of freezing in position, his head and bill pointed straight up to the sky, so that he passes for a sprig of grass or a cattail."

Even so tiny a creature as the ghost crab wins his respect. The adult ghost crab, or fiddler, measuring four inches across, is a pale crustacean that seemingly can vanish before your eyes as it slips into an indentation in the sand.

"Because of its squirrel-like habit of burying tidbits of seaweed and other food, it's one of nature's cultivators. It fertilizes the dune line so that the grass grows higher and catches the blowing sand and stabilizes the dunes."

The refuge established in 1938, is one of the smallest — about 4,600 acres of land and 4,640 acres of water — and one of the most important on the East Coast Flyway.

Duck hunters, too, have become a part of nature's chain of life. The refuge grew out of their concern at the vanishing game birds. They support the sanctuary by buying migratory waterfowl stamps.

"If it wasn't for the refuge, there'd be no birds to shoot. Here they can rest and feed and have a sporting chance to survive," said Waterfield. He was a hunting and fishing guide before he put his lore to work as a biological assistant with the refuge. He hasn't been shooting in nine years.

"I just always find something else to do," he said. He paused to watch a white American egret flap slowly across the marsh.

"Most of the time I have to say at Back Bay Refuge you find something of interest," he said, "most of the time."

There's refuge, too, for the beach's rapidly expanding human population in False Cape Park, next door to the Refuge, and in Seashore State Park, at the other end of the beach.

Cars jam the lot at Seashore's entrance, but 50 feet down the foot trail, the hiker drops out of the 20th Century. After the highway's flash and

glitter his eyes require a few minutes to adjust to the woods' subtleties, but at a tiny rustle he looks down and sees a snake, mottled brown, gray, and yellow, winding away as if a breeze had stirred a line of leaves in motion.

Here and there are ponds, fringed with knobby-kneed cypress trees trailing Spanish moss, gray-bearded old Confederates, all talked out, just musing. Gazing over the cypress-stained water, like the Biblical mirror in which one sees darkly, the walker realizes something is looking at him, steadily, unblinking – a turtle on the end of a log, a snapper big as a skillet, its distended head the handle. At times, indeed, the visitor becomes aware of half a dozen watchful, silent sentries.

The forest carpets 25,000-year-old ridges – dead dunes, they are called – but in one segment are 50-foot high living dunes, hills and deep bowls bare except for fringes of brush, still moving and shaping themselves. They are marching slow motion, inch by inch, like a tractor tread as the wind blows sand up the gentler slope and drops it on the advancing face of the dune, park naturalists point out. In summer temperatures soar above 100 degrees. In winter snowfalls, children sleigh on the dunes, the only hills on Virginia's low doorsill.

Efforts to open the park for development of residential subdivisions and other schemes are constant. The pressure sometimes comes from quarters difficult to resist. In 1970 the State yielded to a request from the City of Virginia Beach and leased 15 acres of the giant dunes as a site for a $1.5 million elementary school. But the city had ample open space elsewhere that was as well or better situated for schools. Environmentalists compelled the State to reverse its decision.

Such episodes bring to mind Balzac's *La Peau de Chagrin,* in which the hero receives a piece of magic skin that insures instant gratification of his every desire. The skin, however, shrinks along with the owner's life span at every wish. As the end nears, he tries, frantically, to no avail, to stretch the bit of skin. Virginia ought never bargain away such patches as Seashore, False Cape, and Back Bay.

Adjoining Seashore State Park is the Fort Story Army Base, site of the amphibious branch of the Army Transportation Corps, overlooking Chesapeake Bay. In the Base atop a 30-foot sand dune is an eight-sided tower of weatherbeaten sandstone, the Cape Henry Lighthouse. Visitors climb the staircase to the top of the 72-foot tower for a gull's-eye view of the coast.

Legend says that bonfires used to guide ships past Cape Henry into Chesapeake Bay, but pirates began to come ashore, capture the beaconkeeper, and build a fire at another spot to lure ships onto sandy shoals, for plundering. In 1790 the first Congress of the United States authorized construction of the slim gray tower, built in 1791. Its watch duty eventually was assumed by another lighthouse

Fisherman has Hampton Road to himself

The busy Roads knows aircraft carriers, cruisers, freighters, and subs, destroyers, tenders, tanker and tugs, but at times a man is alone in his own small boat.

in a striking black and white design, which still stands nearby.

A Norfolk civic leader, Mrs. Frantz Naylor, began campaigning in 1926 to make the United States conscious of the fact that the colonists of 1607 stepped ashore on April 26 at Cape Henry. Among other crusades, she established in Norfolk what was the first school lunch program in the United States.

Mrs. Naylor saw to the building of a permanent stone cross on the dune to mark the area in which the colonists had come ashore and planted a wooden one.

The best time to explore the area is late in the afternoon. Most visitors to the beach pack up their umbrellas and folding chairs about 5 o'clock, straggle to their lodgings—and thereby miss the most beguiling part of the day.

At that hour along the shore line at Cape Henry, the beach is much as it was when the sea-weary settlers splashed ashore for their first look at the brave new world.

A flock of tiny sandpipers scurry in unison at the lacy edges of the waves, as if tied by invisible threads, hunched, looking for food, their images gleaming palely a moment on the slick, wet sand when the waves retreat.

The beach is hard packed at the water line, crunchy as cake crust a little higher, and soft as coarse flour as the visitor begins to climb the steep and shifting dune.

He tends to move sideways up its face to keep his footing, and, concentrating on what's before him, is surprised, pausing for breath, when he looks over his shoulder and finds the sea there, spread out, immense, blue water reaching to blue sky, the long combers marching quick step to the shore, row on row of grenadiers in white shakos, six white lines at a time against the blue.

The sandpipers have been joined by a squad of solemn white gulls, as immobile as chess pieces on a board. An Englishman seeing them might have felt a moment's longing for his hearthside.

There's a strangled cry in the sky, and the climber on the face of the dune looks up, a little frightened, but sees that the bird by the cut of its wing must be a gull, not a roc.

Near the dune's top the going is so steep that he scrambles on hands and knees—the band of colonists that came ashore must have had at least one clumsy fellow — not knowing even today precisely what the view will be, until, topping the rise, he sits panting, looking over a landscape pitchy as the sea the settlers endured for four months, full of dunes and scrub and, far beyond, the dark line of pines and the unknown.

Given, he thinks, a little luck, a lot of work, and a good deal of patience for one another among members of the company, the experiment just might yet work.